THE
SMART
STRATEGY
BOOK

50 WAYS TO SOLVE TRICKY BUSINESS ISSUES

KEVIN DUNCAN

PRAISE FOR
THE SMART STRATEGY BOOK

"Everything starts with a strategy, but knowing where to get started can feel overwhelming. Kevin brings original thought, humour, and wisdom to convert your strategy from a recipe for disaster into a piece of cake."
Paul Davies, Director of Marketing and Audiences, BBC

"As usual the style is sharp and to the point, easy to digest, accessible, and practical. Great quality bite-sized learnings and prompts to action."
Don Williams, Partner, KPMG LLP

"Kevin brings clarity and simplicity to the role strategic and creative thinking can play in solving business problems. If you have a chance to be motivated by Kevin in person, it will be time very well spent."
Enyi Nwosu, Chief Strategy Officer, Universal McCann

"Kevin's is a mind so well-organized, it would be foolish to ignore his wisdom on the subject of strategy. *The Smart Strategy Book* provides just the right amount of guidance in creating valuable and, most importantly, action-oriented strategies."
Richard Morris, CEO IPG Mediabrands, UK & Ireland

Published by
LID Publishing
An imprint of LID Business Media Ltd.
The Record Hall, Studio 304,
16-16a Baldwins Gardens,
London EC1N 7RJ, UK

info@lidpublishing.com
www.lidpublishing.com

A member of:

businesspublishersroundtable.com

© Kevin Duncan, 2022
© LID Business Media Limited, 2022
First edition published in 2018

Printed by Imak Ofset

ISBN: 978-1-911687-22-1
ISBN: 978-1-911687-23-8 (ebook)

Cover and page design: Caroline Li

THE SMART STRATEGY BOOK

50 WAYS TO SOLVE TRICKY BUSINESS ISSUES

KEVIN DUNCAN

MADRID | MEXICO CITY | LONDON
NEW YORK | BUENOS AIRES
BOGOTA | SHANGHAI | NEW DELHI

FOR OTHER TITLES IN THE SERIES...

CONCISE
ADVICE
LAB

SMALL BOOKS: BIG IDEAS

CLEVER CONTENT, DYNAMIC IDEAS, PRACTICAL
SOLUTIONS AND ENGAGING VISUALS –
A CATALYST TO INSPIRE NEW WAYS OF THINKING
AND PROBLEM-SOLVING IN A COMPLEX WORLD

conciseadvicelab.com

CONTENTS

PREFACE

Kevin Duncan reads business books. A *lot* of them. More than most business people could read in 11 lifetimes. And, best of all, he can write entertainingly about them.

Here he highlights ideas from 57 fascinating books – a veritable Cook's tour of business insights. Influential authors stand shoulder to shoulder and cheek by jowl: Thaler and Sunstein next to Lafley and Martin; Radjou and Prabhu next to Dixon and Adamson; Downes and Nunes next to Goffee and Jones. You'll find Sinek, Godin, and Gladwell; Lencioni, Kahnemann, and Trott; the Heath brothers, Bannerman, and Pink. It's interesting to see what happens when the best ideas of each bump against those of the others. They seem to produce offspring.

Duncan is superb at pulling out the most telling details. Paraphrasing from Greg McKeown's *Essentialism*, he says that if your commercial strategy boils down to a number, then the chances are it isn't one. Strategists who don't take time to think, he says, are merely planners.

Each chapter contains the essence of one or two well-regarded books. First he sums up the author(s)' wisdom, then he adds his own thoughts – always delightfully opinionated – in the form of a 'Smart Strategy Warning'.

Speaking through his favourite authors, Duncan pokes holes in a lot of brightly coloured business balloons. Take, for example: Most things aren't worth doing. All models are wrong. Ignorance has tremendous value. Do everything at once. A disadvantage is an advantage. Most market research is flawed. Leaders eat last. And possibly my favourite – antelopes don't have hobbies.

You'll learn how to zoom in, zoom out, and 'ooch' your way to a workable theory. With experience, you'll begin to recognize the 'caramba moment', and on the way learn to avoid the perils of 'WYSIATI' (What You See Is All There Is). You'll soon be harnessing the power of 'clevers' and using 'service recovery' to turn mistakes into customer loyalty.

I won't spoil the adventure for you. Dip in, dip out, let the ideas bump together. Who says strategy has to be boring?

Marty Neumeier
Author of *Scramble: A Business Thriller*

INTRODUCTION

It's always fun to review a book five years on.

The author never quite knows what the public reaction to a book might be, so it's good to report that this one has been well received, particularly when training hundreds of people.

Strategy is a much-abused subject.

An online search of the word alone produces over 2 billion references, so a lot of people are interested in it.

A similar search on a popular retail site shows that there are over 120,000 books written about it.

So, there is no shortage of opinion on the topic, but are they any help?

How many times have you bought an earnest book on strategy and not finished it because it was too long-winded?

My intention here is to get you to intelligent solutions, quickly.

A good strategy needs to be short, clear, and easy to understand.

Smart and original, if possible.

This book offers 50 ideas to help you arrive at decent strategic thinking as quickly as possible, and presents it in a way that we can all understand.

It covers seven of the most common strategic areas that affect businesses: commercial, brand, customer, sales, people, innovation, and communication.

Be aware, however, that this is not a method where you slavishly follow the steps in a sequence.

In fact, some of the suggestions may seem to contradict each other. That's intentional – giving the reader many different perspectives from which to look at the business challenge.

All the approaches here have a use in one context or another, and have been tested many times on real business problems.

Overall, it means getting the initial big idea right, working all the way through every aspect of what the product or service can do, and then explaining it well.

Find some new angles for your thinking, and don't forget to heed the smart strategy warnings at the end of each idea, because the whole area is fraught with pitfalls.

Good luck, and let me know how you get on.

Kevin Duncan
Westminster, 2022

IDEA 1: WHAT IS STRATEGY, ANYWAY?

This book looks at seven strategic areas, with seven suggested approaches in each part. So that's 49 possible approaches.

But there is one thing that underpins them all: a clear definition of what strategy truly is.

A strategy is a plan of action designed to achieve a long-term or overall aim.

It is what you have decided to do.

That's it.

If anyone tries to tell you it's more complicated than that, then they are trying to mislead you.

There are many areas where a decent strategy will be of use.

Here I have tried to cover the most universal themes:
- **Commercial**: is it going to make money?
- **Brand**: have we created a good one that people want to be associated with?
- **Customer**: do we have a plan to reach them effectively?
- **Sales**: can we generate enough and, if so, how?

- **People**: how will our staff make all this thinking happen?
- **Innovation**: can we come up with intelligent new ideas to help growth?
- **Communication**: how will we explain all of this to colleagues, staff and customers?

All of this should be explainable on one sheet of paper, and sometimes even on a postcard.

What a strategy is not:
- a long-winded discourse
- a series of impenetrable charts
- a drawing of the Parthenon populated by a long list of adjectives
- a series of tactics cobbled together to suggest a unified thought
- a verb, as in 'to strategize'.

A strategy states intention and direction in such a clear way that everybody knows what they are doing.

So that's point number one. Now let's look at the other 49.

A NOTE ON THE MILITARY METAPHOR

Another definition of strategy is the art of planning and directing military operations.

Sadly, this has led to an unfortunate overuse of macho terms in the business world.

Tasks are often described as mission critical, and businesses are forever seeking the so-called magic bullet.

As well as strategy and tactics, customers are subjected to campaigns, viewed as targets, and sent mailshots.

But business is not really about world domination, is it?

So you won't find any language of that sort in this book.

A WORD ON COMMERCIAL STRATEGY

This section is all about the big stuff.

That's the direction of an entire company, organization, product or service.

Amazingly, some companies stumble along without ever writing this down or agreeing it at board level.

So the commercial strategy is always the place to start.

Without it, every other type of strategy could be trying to enact the wrong thing.

It is often quite serious, but it doesn't have to be pompous.

It is primarily concerned with what the company does and how it makes money.

The biggest sin that can be committed here is to include too much, make it unnecessarily complicated, become long-winded or indulge in fanciful thinking.

It needs to be short and clear, so that everyone can understand it.

It is essential that the strategy is free of bullshit, so that it includes no corporate self-delusion.

It is categorically *not* about the detail.

All that comes later.

PART ONE

COMMERCIAL
STRATEGY

1. STRATEGY IS CHOICE

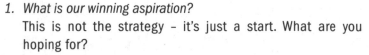

According to Lafley and Martin, authors of *Playing to Win*, strategy is not complex, but it is hard, because of the pain of having to make choices.

The five crucial strategic choices they identify are:

1. *What is our winning aspiration?*
   This is not the strategy – it's just a start. What are you hoping for?

2. *Where will we play?*
   Choose the markets, categories and product areas where you can compete effectively. Exclusions are helpful – don't start multiple wars against competitors when you can't win.

3. *How will we win in our chosen markets?*
   Look at cost and differentiation. Is the company or the product as good as you think it is? Many business people have a rose-tinted view of their own products and overestimate their potential.

4. *What capabilities must be in place to win?*
   Create an activity system that will do the job. If the company can't currently do this, look carefully at required resources and investment.

5. *What management systems are required to support our choice?*
   Has the company or department got the right grown-ups at the top, enough staff to get everything done and a system to make it all work?

Make those decisions and you'll have made a start on a decent commercial strategy.

SMART STRATEGY WARNING

Making everything a priority is a big mistake. Strategy is all about choosing one thing over others. If your strategy runs to a huge document or presentation including everything plus the kitchen sink, then it probably won't work. If you try to do it all, you won't achieve any of it.

If you are about to write a strategy, limit yourself to one page. If you have already written one, take a highlighter pen and use only the best bits. Then redraft it on one page. Smart strategy is clear and simple.

2. THINK BEFORE YOU PLAN

Strategy expert Max McKeown believes that thinking *before* you plan is vital. Strategists who don't take time to think are just planners.

Strategy is all about shaping the future, and that requires a combination of thinking, planning and reacting to events that will undoubtedly emerge along the way. The crucial questions are:

- What do we want to do?
- What do we think is possible?
- What do we need to do to achieve our goals?
- When should we react to new opportunities and adapt plans?

Inspiration and insight can be drawn from looking forwards, backwards and outwards, which often means blending smart prediction with past experience and astute observation of what's happening outside the company and the market category.

Strategists need to know what stage their company, industry, products and services have reached. What crises have they survived? What will be next?

Survival is a priority, but growth is better. Crucial questions here are:

- How has the company grown in the past?
- What could fuel it in the future?
- Which markets and products could offer the greatest potential?

Just doing what you did last year isn't imaginative enough. This wide-ranging questioning must come before any semblance of a plan is constructed.

SMART STRATEGY WARNING

Don't just dive in and write a plan. Many individuals and companies are fooled by plans. They think that because it is written down in an impressive way, then it must be a good strategy. This is sometimes called the 'spurious authority of type'. Somehow it all seems more convincing when it's typed up.

But that doesn't mean the strategy is any good. If you are drafting a strategy, use a pen and paper. The very last thing you should do is to make it look pretty. Are you staring at a strategy that looks impressive but lacks proper substance? If so, rip it up and think of something more original and effective.

3. PURSUE PRINCIPLES, NOT MONEY

If your commercial strategy boils down to a number, then the chances are it isn't a strategy.

"Grow the business by 10%" is not a strategy. Nor is "Acquire *x* number of customers."

Each of these might be an objective or a desired outcome, but they're not the means by which you will get there.

Strategy has been described as "the hard art of standing apart". That means having integrity and a clear sense of purpose – a noble, unwavering belief that translates into firm principles for how to conduct your business.

It means being distinctive, standing for something and doing what you say you will. None of which is easy.

In his book *Essentialism*, Greg McKeown explains the components of an 'essential intent'. It needs to be both inspirational and concrete.

For example, a vision or mission can be inspirational, but it is rarely concrete.

Quarterly objectives are concrete but never inspirational.

Values are neither, and so are usually both general and bland.

Inspiration isn't hard to identify, but it takes bravery.

The key to a concrete strategy is answering the question: "How will we know when we're done?"

"A laptop for every child in Africa" is both concrete and inspirational.

Good strategy pursues principles rather than just money.

⚠ SMART STRATEGY WARNING

It is important to avoid any wishful thinking. For a strategy to really mean something, it will most likely embrace elements of sacrifice (what the company or brand won't do) and be genuine. You can only do that if your strategy captures the imagination and is expressed well.

If the strategy is based on a number, it is probably ill-conceived. Numbers are not motivating in their own right. Start by getting the intent of the company or brand right and, if the strategy is a good one, the numbers will follow.

4. WIDEN OPTIONS, ATTAIN DISTANCE

If you are going to be strategically decisive, then you need to widen your options, reality-test your assumptions, attain distance before deciding and prepare to be wrong.

That's the advice of experts Chip and Dan Heath.

Stage 1 entails avoiding a narrow time frame, multitracking (considering more than one option simultaneously), and finding someone who has already solved your problem. Give yourself time, look at lots of possibilities and take wide-ranging advice, from outside the company if needed.

Stage 2 involves considering doing the opposite, zooming in and zooming out between the big picture and the detail, and 'ooching' – a Southern US word for running small experiments to test theories.

Stage 3 includes overcoming short-term emotion and honouring your core priorities. Pragmatic, fact-based thinking works, not so-called gut feel, whatever that may be.

Stage 4 is bookending the future – mapping out a range of outcomes from very bad to very good – and setting up tripwires to provide sufficient early warning of adjustments throughout the year.

All of this takes time, so you can't just knock up a strategy in a day.

Consider the widest range of possibilities.

Test the robustness of your proposed strategy with a quick pilot, then take the emotion out of it and prepare to be wrong.

If you are wrong, then you may have to go through the whole thing again to get it right.

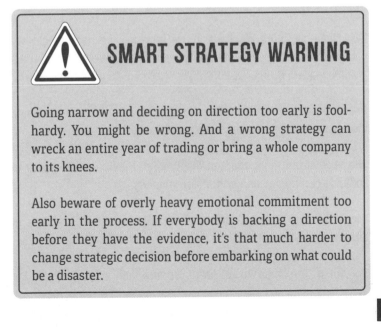

⚠ SMART STRATEGY WARNING

Going narrow and deciding on direction too early is fool-hardy. You might be wrong. And a wrong strategy can wreck an entire year of trading or bring a whole company to its knees.

Also beware of overly heavy emotional commitment too early in the process. If everybody is backing a direction before they have the evidence, it's that much harder to change strategic decision before embarking on what could be a disaster.

5. REMOVE SILOS

The word 'silo' comes from the Greek word *siros*, meaning 'corn pit'.

The meaning moved across to military missile silos, and then to systems and departments that work in isolation. Synonyms include 'ghettos', 'buckets' and 'tribes'.

Businesses should strive to prevent silos in the first place or work hard to remove them.

Ever since civilized society began, we have felt the need to classify, categorize, and specialize. This can make things more efficient and help give the leaders in organizations a sense of confidence that all is well.

But it can also create a 'structural fog', with the full picture of where the organization is heading hidden from view.

Silos are rife in many modern institutions. They have the power to collapse companies and destabilize markets.

They blind and confuse, often making companies act in risky and damaging ways.

So, when it comes to devising appropriate strategies, putting everything in its so-called place isn't always such a bright idea.

No single part of a company should determine the strategy of the company – and that includes the strategy department, if there is one.

Team boundaries should be kept flexible and fluid, so that information flows effectively, ensuring that knowledge is truly shared.

The golden rule when generating an effective commercial strategy is: *ask everyone first.*

All companies have pockets of expertise, and their knowledge is often priceless.

It's often the people who know the most who say the least, so make sure you use their knowledge.

⚠ SMART STRATEGY WARNING

Strategies developed solely by strategists are often unsuccessful. Strategists and strategy departments do not have a monopoly on strategy. So, coming up with a strategy in an ivory tower is a cardinal sin.

Before drawing first thoughts together, make sure you visit all corners of the business, solicit opinion, and ask open-ended questions. Be open-minded. Consider many possibilities. Put an eclectic working team together and kick ideas around.

6. UNCOMMON SENSE VS. COMMON NONSENSE

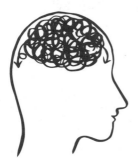

There is 'common nonsense' behind much managerial behaviour today, particularly in the tired and cynical assumptions that underpin routines, rituals and discussions.

That's the view of Jules Goddard and Tony Eccles in their counter-cultural book *Uncommon Sense, Common Nonsense*.

'Uncommon sense' is what differentiates smart companies from the others and allows them to rise above 'common nonsense'.

Too many strategic decisions rely on a HIPPO (a **H**ighly **P**aid **P**erson's **O**pinion).

Management strategy models biased in favour of control, at the expense of learning, tend to involve:
- *Best practice*: the recipe for formulaic sameness
- *Operational excellence*: 'doorknob polishing' pedestrian policies
- *Competitive benchmarking*: plagiarism run riot
- *Balanced scorecards*: the bureaucrat's revenge
- *Performance targets*: insults for the conscientious
- *Annual budgets*: the pathology of under-ambition
- *Financial incentives*: bribes for loners and cynics

- ***Organizational alignment***: fear of diversity
- ***Shared values***: the extinction of individualism
- ***Professional standards***: box-ticking for the risk averse
- ***Charismatic leadership***: narcissism unbound.

None of this contributes one jot to a decent strategy. It's all administration and involves no original thought.

No business sets out to impoverish shareholders, irritate customers, demoralize employees, outrage governments and leave the world worse off – so why write mission statements and strategies that claim otherwise?

Uncommon sense in business is, by definition, uncommon.

Make sure your strategy includes plenty of it and no common nonsense.

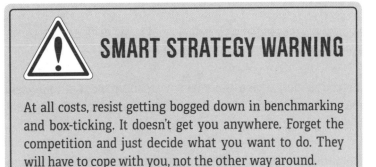

⚠ SMART STRATEGY WARNING

At all costs, resist getting bogged down in benchmarking and box-ticking. It doesn't get you anywhere. Forget the competition and just decide what you want to do. They will have to cope with you, not the other way around.

Cut out all the management bollocks and come up with something intelligent, pithy and inspiring. You'll probably need just the one page.

7. FIND YOUR NEMO

Strategy is choice, so you can't have it all.

There can only be one strategy.

Knocking up a plan before you have thought it through will not generate a strategy.

You first need to widen your options and attain distance, otherwise you could be too close to the subject

You can't simply sit and generate a blistering strategy at your desk. You need to remove silos and draw from the widest possible pool of expertise.

And it doesn't pay to dwell on limitations. Instead, turn these to your advantage by thinking more laterally.

In his book *Business Genius*, James Bannerman suggests that to focus properly on the matter in hand, it can help to try the NEMO technique.

It stands for "**N**othing **E**lse **M**atters except the **0**," where you picture the 0 as the bull's-eye of an archery target.

This is what you are aiming for – your purpose. It should be the one single thing that the strategy represents.

Just the one thing.

Strategies with multiple purposes don't work.

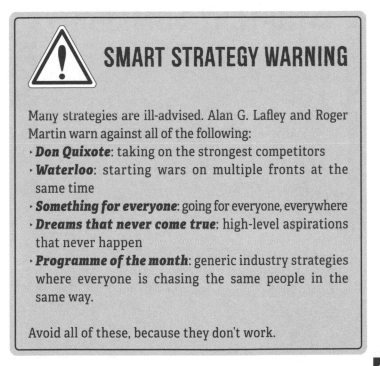

SMART STRATEGY WARNING

Many strategies are ill-advised. Alan G. Lafley and Roger Martin warn against all of the following:

- *Don Quixote*: taking on the strongest competitors
- *Waterloo*: starting wars on multiple fronts at the same time
- *Something for everyone*: going for everyone, everywhere
- *Dreams that never come true*: high-level aspirations that never happen
- *Programme of the month*: generic industry strategies where everyone is chasing the same people in the same way.

Avoid all of these, because they don't work.

SMART COMMERCIAL STRATEGY SUMMARY

- Strategy is choice.
- Think before you plan.
- Pursue principles, not money.
- Widen your options and attain distance.
- Remove silos.
- Uncommon sense v. common nonsense.
- Find your NEMO.

A WORD ON BRAND STRATEGY

Once the commercial strategy has been agreed,
it is time to turn your attention to what the brand stands for.

In many cases, a company will have a whole range of brands,
in which case it is particularly important to understand
and articulate the differences between them.

Reviewing an entire portfolio of brands could reveal
unnecessary duplication or messy overlaps.

The world of brands and branding is a box of bombs.

This world is open to considerable abuse and is the subject
of regular derision, much of it self-inflicted.

Many of us have sat in countless meetings with so-called
brand guardians, staring at an 80-chart presentation
filled with impenetrable constructs.

These presentations very often purport to contain the so-called
'essence of the brand'. They are often a blur of brand onions,
pyramids, pillars, values, visions and hundreds of generic
adjectives. But where do they get us?

They're enough to make you grab your coat and head for the door.

It doesn't have to be that way.

An effective brand strategy needs to clearly articulate
what the current position of the brand is and how it
intends to develop in a certain direction.

It is possible to generate a bullshit-free brand strategy
that is distinctive and helpful.

Let's see how.

PART TWO

BRAND
STRATEGY

1. GAP IN THE MARKET VS. MARKET IN THE GAP

Devising an effective brand strategy requires careful thought and dispassionate analysis. Enthusiasm for the fate of the brand is admirable, but hyperbolic language that overemphasizes the capabilities of the brand is not.

Too many strategists exaggerate the possibilities available to a brand, but they would be better off being realistic.

The first thing to do is map the market.

Start by selecting the two most important factors in the market, then plot two perpendicular axes (one for each factor) from high to low and place your brand and any competitors on the grid.

Use the results to identify gaps in the market or significant overlaps.

Being out on your own could either be good (more distinctive) or bad (in the wrong territory). Being with too many other brands is usually too cluttered, just like schoolchildren all chasing a ball.

But beware fool's gold. Fool's gold looks like gold, but it isn't. It is usually some other yellow mineral, such as pyrite or chalcopyrite.

White space is blank, and when it's on a strategist's market map, it makes them think that there's a gap to be exploited.

But they might be wrong.

There is apparently a gap in the market, but is there a market in the gap?

Brand strategists need to ponder this question very carefully before making recommendations too hastily.

The apparent gap could simply be a failure masquerading as a viable opportunity.

SMART STRATEGY WARNING

Many strategists knock up a market map and triumphantly declare that they have spotted a gap in the market. But they might be too hasty – and wrong. After generating this initial view of the brand position, good strategists must ask two vital questions: (1) Why is this space unoccupied? and (2) What do others know that we don't?

The so-called gap may be there for a very good reason, so look carefully at the flaws of that position in the market and at any previous attempts by competitors to occupy that area. Chances are someone has made the same mistake already, so you can avoid it.

2. INVESTIGATE THE UNINTERESTING

If you want to make a brand distinctive, you will most likely have to look at things you haven't automatically considered before. So an exploratory phase at the start is vital.

It is also essential if you have been working on the same brand for a long time. If so, your strategy may have become repetitive, relying on formulaic old ways and losing its effectiveness on the way.

It's at this point that the smart brand strategist will take on a new lease of life and investigate different areas.

Identifying and investigating the areas we are *not* naturally interested in massively multiplies the number of new connections we can make, according to Dave Trott in his book *One Plus One Equals Three.*

Ignorance has a tremendous value.

If you don't know what apparently can't be done, then you can think freely.

This gives you much greater strategic freedom and allows you to unshackle yourself from samey thinking.

Your next step is to question the question posed by the brief, or by the strategic challenge that has been set.

Before you rush to suggested solutions, what precisely is the brand challenge?

Answer that and you may progress much faster or arrive in a completely different place.

Reinterpreting the brief is often solving the problem.

⚠ SMART STRATEGY WARNING

Many brand strategists simply dive in and invent a strategy. That's not very smart. There will be many things that they haven't looked at. A good start would be to list all the old assumptions and beliefs, and check whether they are still any help.

Next, consider looking at a whole range of outlying issues and material that has been disregarded to date. There may be a gem of an insight lurking there somewhere. Don't simply fall back on what you are comfortable or familiar with – cast the net much wider. You may surprise yourself and your colleagues.

3. CHANGE THE PROBLEM

When a brand is struggling or needs a lift, try changing the problem you can't solve into one that you can.

Many brand strategists look at situations they can't seem to solve and are then stumped.

But *form follows function*, so you need to get the brief right first, and then the rest of the thinking will flow properly.

Many customers and clients come to strategists saying, "I don't know what I want, but I'll know it when I see it."

Or they may request a prescriptive formula, such as: "I want an *x*."

The first request is hopelessly vague (no brief at all) and the second narrowly specific (and probably wrong).

Nothing exists in limbo and context is everything, so you need to out-think the problem by changing a piece of it.

"Why?" is the most important word you will ever use and the best question you can ever ask.

Too many strategists accept what appears to be in front of them.

There are lessons to be learned here from behavioural economics. As Daniel Kahneman points out in his book *Thinking, Fast and Slow*, the 'affect heuristic' involves people making judgements based on their emotions.

The question "How do I feel about it?" becomes a surrogate for a much harder question: "What do I think about it?"

On balance, strategists need to think more than they feel.

Otherwise they become victims of WYSIATI (What you see is all there is), which involves jumping to conclusions based on limited evidence.

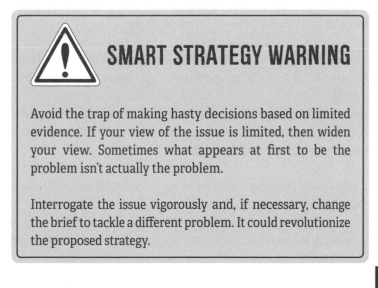

⚠️ SMART STRATEGY WARNING

Avoid the trap of making hasty decisions based on limited evidence. If your view of the issue is limited, then widen your view. Sometimes what appears at first to be the problem isn't actually the problem.

Interrogate the issue vigorously and, if necessary, change the brief to tackle a different problem. It could revolutionize the proposed strategy.

4. DOUBT EVERYTHING

Doubt everything, probe, diverge, converge and re-evaluate relentlessly.

That's the advice of Brabandere and Iny, authors of *Thinking in New Boxes*.

So-called thinking 'outside the box' isn't the answer. True ingenuity needs structure, hard analysis and bold brainstorming. That means thinking in new boxes.

A box is a mental model – a construction that exists purely within you and that dictates how you view the world.

Inductive thinking involves moving from observed fragmented details to a connected view, a binding principle, a hypothesis or a strategic box.

Deductive thinking involves applying such a framework to observed details to see whether the box has the capacity to interpret them. Logic is the science of deduction.

Prospective thinking asks: What might or could happen? What should I do about it?

A *eureka moment* is when you suddenly realize how to shift your perception.

A **caramba moment** is when you realize one or more of your boxes (set of assumptions) are out of date. As you probably know, *caramba* is a Spanish expression of surprise.

Re-examine your approach to brand strategy in five steps:
1. **Doubt everything**: challenge your current perspectives.
2. **Probe the possible**: explore the options around you.
3. **Diverge**: generate many new and exciting ideas, even if they seem absurd.
4. **Converge**: evaluate and select ideas that will drive breakthrough results.
5. **Re-evaluate**: relentlessly. No idea is good forever.

⚠ SMART STRATEGY WARNING

Many brand strategies fail to ask at the outset what is currently taken for granted. Prospective thinking asks:
- What might or could happen?
- What should I do about it?
- What working practices should be challenged and possibly changed?

Describe your company or product using five words. Now try doing it without those words. You may create a new box or way of thinking that could have a significant bearing on your brand strategy.

5. MESSINESS = UNEXPECTED LINKS

A good strategy for a brand doesn't emerge from a slow linear process.

You need to leave things a bit messy so that unexpected links can be made.

Contrary to what tidy-minded people suggest, if you want to be creative, you may need a little more disorder in your world.

Openness and adaptability are inherently *messy*, as stressed by Tim Harford in his book of the same name.

Strategists with 'weak filters' can get easily distracted, but they are actually more creative, because they take in more stimuli.

Frustration and distraction often help us to solve strategic problems because we are determined to find a better way. Tension can be beneficial.

If you are working in a strategy team, messy teamwork actually gets more done because it throws up more possibilities.

Interestingly, tidy offices don't work very well because people who work in them feel disempowered.

Empowered offices are 30% more productive, and people flourish when they control their own space.

A messy desk can help too. In the battle between so-called 'filers' and 'pilers', the pilers win, because they keep less and regularly ditch material when there is too much on their desk. In contrast, filers have so much stuff that they often can't find things.

All of this adds up to what scientist Stuart Kauffman calls the 'adjacent possible' – the nearest next steps that can be made.

Leaving things a bit messy opens up many possibilities and may allow you to spot the most fertile next steps.

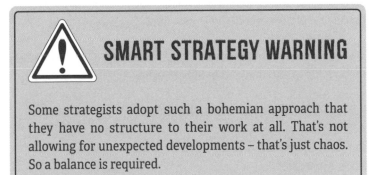

⚠ SMART STRATEGY WARNING

Some strategists adopt such a bohemian approach that they have no structure to their work at all. That's not allowing for unexpected developments – that's just chaos. So a balance is required.

Simply being haphazard won't necessarily lead to anything. Examine the sameness of how things usually are, and then deliberately ignite some interesting new interactions to stimulate new thought. Think outside the company too.

6. MOST THINGS AREN'T WORTH DOING

In his book *Essentialism*, Greg McKeown espouses the disciplined pursuit of less.

The non-essentialist is all things to all people, pursues everything in an undisciplined way and lives a life that does not satisfy. He or she thinks that almost everything is essential.

The essentialist does less but better, creating a life that really matters. He or she thinks that almost everything is non-essential.

If it isn't a clear yes, then it's a clear no.

To create a coherent and clear brand strategy, concentrate only on what is essential.

Eliminate everything that has no bearing on the essential task.

In a 'reverse pilot', you test whether removing an initiative or activity will have any negative consequences. Doing this regularly reduces workload and eases the burden on crucial resources.

'Minimal viable progress' is the smallest amount useful to the essential task. Consider doing no more than this so that the brand can focus its complete attention on one helpful thing.

The word 'priority' came into the English language in the 1400s. It was singular, and it meant the very first or prior thing.

Only in the 1900s did we turn it into a plural and start talking about 'priorities'. Now we have too many of them.

7. COPY SOMETHING

One of the most effective ways to draw inspiration for a decent brand strategy is to copy something else. Innovation is 80–90% known stuff, with a 10–20% twist.

It's not where you get it from – it's where you take it to.

The principle of 'category stealing' is simple: choose a category different from your own and ask how companies and brands in that category would approach your issue.

Everyone operates in one category or another, and many of the traditions, rituals and formats in them operate in quite fixed ways. This can lead to sameness in one sector, but could provide inspiration in another.

As behavioural expert Mark Earls points out in his book *Copy, Copy, Copy*, copying is to be cherished, if it is approached in the right way.

Copying strategies really works, so you can do smarter marketing by using other people's ideas.

Look to successes elsewhere and apply them to your issue.

Tight 'single white copying' (named after the film *Single White Female*) is no good for innovation because it just slavishly repeats what's been done before.

Copying loosely works better and allows for error and variation.

Questions that provide early rangefinders for progress are:
- What kind of thing is this?
- What kind of solutions might be appropriate?
- What might that look like?

This iterative way of investigating strategies is far more fluid and informative than detailed planning, and allows you to move much more quickly.

⚠ SMART STRATEGY WARNING

You can't just steal another strategy and apply it lock, stock and barrel, especially if the brand in question is a competitor. What you are looking for are analogies and inspiration from an area a little way off the path the brand is currently on.

Think widely and identify norms elsewhere that could inspire a new strategy in your sector.

SMART BRAND STRATEGY SUMMARY

- Is there a market in the gap?
- Investigate the uninteresting.
- Change the problem.
- Doubt everything.
- Messiness = unexpected links.
- Most things aren't worth doing.
- Copy something.

A WORD ON CUSTOMER STRATEGY

You can be the best-organized company in the world, have the most advanced products and use amazing branding, but, without customers, a company amounts to nothing.

So it pays to have an excellent customer strategy.

However, many strategies are found wanting when it comes to their candid depiction of customers and exactly where they are going to come from.

Many are described as 'consumers' – as though they eat the product.

Many are categorized as 'target audiences' – as though you can fire things at them.

Some are clustered into imaginary and often condescending typologies – 'Deborah from Walthamstow', anyone?

Much of this work is too fanciful and conveniently ignores the stark reality that a customer is just someone who buys your stuff.

And their behaviour can be very hard to predict.

Let's have a look at what robust customer strategy really should involve.

PART THREE

CUSTOMER STRATEGY

1. MISLEADING RESEARCH

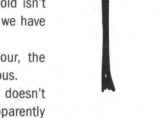

Most market research is flawed because customers can't provide accurate answers even if they wanted to. This is because:

- Much of the information we hold isn't consciously processed, nor do we have conscious access to it.
- The more routine the behaviour, the more it is likely to be unconscious.
- The absence of knowledge doesn't stop us from providing an apparently sensible rationale after the event.
- Our unconscious filters aren't understood by our conscious mind, so we can't even accurately report what influenced us.

We also tell ourselves myths, so group discussions and surveys removed from the moment don't work. Live testing in the moment gets the closest to replicating real life.

Research is perceived as a means of reducing the inherent risk in decision-making, so everyone wants to believe the findings, true or not.

Unfortunately, there are many reasons that most questions should be avoided, because often they can:

- Inadvertently tell people what to think about
- Change what people think
- Unintentionally lead the witness
- Accidentally sell
- End up persuading people to like something.

Artificially deconstructing the consumer experience is often misleading, so people's responses can't always be trusted, even though they are offered in good faith.

The good news is that the science behind why we buy can now mainly be explained.

And that's the subject of the next section.

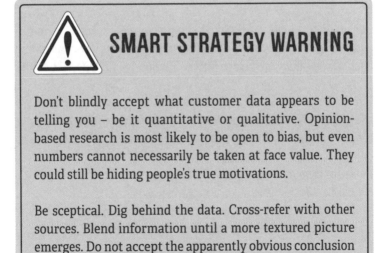

SMART STRATEGY WARNING

Don't blindly accept what customer data appears to be telling you – be it quantitative or qualitative. Opinion-based research is most likely to be open to bias, but even numbers cannot necessarily be taken at face value. They could still be hiding people's true motivations.

Be sceptical. Dig behind the data. Cross-refer with other sources. Blend information until a more textured picture emerges. Do not accept the apparently obvious conclusion until it has been rigorously examined.

2. THE THINKING/ DOING GAP

Decision science is not smoke and mirrors. It can be applied in a practical way if properly understood.

Our autopilot (implicit, system 1) has a far greater bearing on our purchasing decisions than many think. Behavioural economics has been saying this for some time. This is effortless, automatic, fast action.

The pilot (explicit, system 2) is the rational, apparently controlled process that is usually mentioned in research as a reason to buy, but this is often misleading since people can't even explain it themselves.

There are three main purchasing principles:
- *Tangibility*: tangible signals trigger heuristics.
- *Immediacy*: the autopilot prefers immediate rewards, not future ones.
- *Certainty*: the autopilot prefers the safe, certain choice.

Purchasing involves a decision between reward (ownership) and pain (price). The brain offsets the two to create a 'net value'. For example, price lists with no pound signs sell more because monetary symbols trigger pain signals.

It is possible to change behaviour without changing minds, usually by changing the 'decision interface' – the context at the moment of purchase.

Triggering 'process endowment' is also important – people are more likely to purchase again with a loyalty card showing some stamps already filled in because they feel that they are already underway.

Contrary to what many strategists would have us believe, brain science shows that customers do not regard brands as people.

Their reactions are dictated by the brain part that deals with physical objects – a bit of a kick in the teeth for the "If your brand were a person ..." school.

 SMART STRATEGY WARNING

There is a gap between what people say and what they really think, and between what they think and what they actually do. Effective customer strategy needs to understand how this works.

Avoid viewing customer behaviour as black and white, and don't assume that a seemingly authoritative customer strategy will indeed get people to do what you want. The reality is probably going to be subtler than that.

3. DISLOYAL LOYALISTS

In *The Effortless Experience*, authors Dixon, Toman and DeLisi reject the idea that delighting customers increases loyalty as plain wrong.

In fact, it's all to do with delivering what the brand says, solving basic problems and minimizing customer effort.

All the data in the book comes from a massive survey of nearly 100,000 customers. It asked three questions:
- To what extent does customer service matter in driving customer loyalty?
- What are the things that customer service can do to drive customer loyalty?
- How can customer service improve loyalty while also reducing operating costs?

The main findings were:
- A strategy of delight doesn't pay.
- Satisfaction is not a predictor of loyalty.
- Customer service interactions tend to drive *disloyalty*, not loyalty.
- The key to mitigating disloyalty is reducing customer effort.

Loyalty has three types: repurchase, share of wallet and advocacy.

The survey found that 60 to 80% of customers who defect were satisfied or very satisfied at the last survey. While 96% of customers who have high-effort experiences become disloyal, only 9% with low-effort experiences do. So the role of customer service should be to reduce customer effort.

Customers define high-effort experiences in many ways, including taking more than one contact to resolve a problem, generic service, having to repeat information and being transferred on helplines.

Bad word of mouth has additional power: 45% of those with positive things to say about a company tell three other people, whereas 48% with negative things to say tell ten other people.

In short, customers who at first appear loyal in survey data may be prepared to leave the brand very soon.

 SMART STRATEGY WARNING

Avoid grandiose phrasing such as 'delighting customers' and 'exceeding customer expectations'. They are mainly fanciful hot air and, in many cases, they don't even work. Consider that, in many categories, the absence of interaction with a brand is preferable to having to engage with it.

Don't overstate customer loyalty levels: in most cases they are not loyal to one brand, but to many of them, so they can switch away from yours immediately if conditions change.

4. CAN'T GET NO SATISFACTION

Satisfaction data can be horribly misleading. Many a marketer has sat smugly staring at a set of figures and concluding that all is well when that might not be the case.

Around 80% of 'satisfied' customers will use a different supplier next time, and 96% of unhappy customers won't tell the organization about it. They'll tell their friends instead.

Most customer feedback systems ask the wrong questions in the wrong way and have return rates of less than 15%, so customers typically do not feel engaged or loyal. Moreover, 68% of customer defections are because of 'perceived indifference'.

Customer satisfaction is actually a poor predictor of behaviour – commitment is better. Loyalty is what customers *do*. Commitment is what they *feel* – a much more powerful component.

Customers can appear deceptively loyal but actually be uncommitted. They might only use the brand because everyone else does or through lack of choice, affordability or just distribution.

According to Hofmeyr and Rice, product users can be 'committed' (entrenched or average) or 'uncommitted' (shallow or convertible). Non-users can be 'open' (available or ambivalent) or 'unavailable' (weakly or strongly).

So apparently 'satisfied' customers may be very prepared to leave your brand. A 'last straw' can make a committed user snap and switch to another.

The moment is hard to predict, the decision is usually irreversible, and, to cap it all, these users tend to become missionaries *against* the brand. Strategists beware.

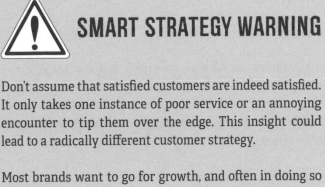

⚠ SMART STRATEGY WARNING

Don't assume that satisfied customers are indeed satisfied. It only takes one instance of poor service or an annoying encounter to tip them over the edge. This insight could lead to a radically different customer strategy.

Most brands want to go for growth, and often in doing so they neglect their existing customer base. Although it may sound less sexy, an objective of customer retention, with a suitable strategy to match, could end up being more cost effective. It costs much more to win a new customer than to keep an existing one.

5. PANIC-FREE SERVICE RECOVERY

Service is an act of help or assistance. To be servile is to be obsequious in attitude or behaviour, or plain submissive.

Decent brands provide top-quality customer service without being servile.

If you've got customers, then you are in a service industry.

Ideally, nothing would ever go wrong, but things go wrong all the time.

It's what you do *when something goes wrong* that makes all the difference.

This is called service recovery.

Customers who have been successfully recovered are 14 times more loyal than those who have never had anything go wrong.

So, perversely, mistakes can fall in the brand's favour, so there's no need to panic when they happen.

Your customers can become ambassadors or cynics, depending on how your brand handles these tricky moments.

The internet has made this phenomenon faster and practically limitless.

Bad news cannot be swept under the carpet – it needs immediate attention, so you need a service recovery strategy to nip it in the bud and solve problems immediately.

It is over six times more expensive to win a new customer than it is to persuade an existing customer to return, so devise a strategy to keep customers happy, especially when things go wrong.

SMART STRATEGY WARNING

Many brands kid themselves that everything will be fine or that their service is great. It may not be. Start by admitting that there are very likely to be some tricky moments, recognize them for what they are likely to be, and put in place an appropriate service recovery process.

Make sure the design of this process tells the customer what's happening, informs colleagues what's happening, chooses the right method of communicating, and doesn't promise things that you can't deliver. Manage their expectations in a sensible and realistic manner, finish on a positive note, and you may have stronger customer loyalty as a result.

6. CUSTOMERS MAKE STRANGE DECISIONS

As the discipline of behavioural economics explains, most people will make irrational decisions if left to their own devices.

A decent customer strategy should use the new science of choice architecture to nudge people towards decisions that will improve their lives, assuming that the brand does indeed help people in some way.

If by any chance the brand you are working on doesn't, then consider resigning.

If we take 'humanness' as a given, we can better understand how people think and we can design environments that make it easier for others to choose what is best for them. We can give them a nudge in the right direction without restricting freedom of choice.

The ability to be so apparently 'smart and dumb' at the same time can be attributed to our automatic system (instinctive rather than actively thinking) versus our reflective system (more deliberate and self-conscious).

In their book *Nudge,* Thaler and Sunstein offer six suggestions as to how to nudge people successfully, complete with a rather dubious accompanying acronym:

- *i**N**centives*: people have to feel they are getting something for their choice.
- *Understand mappings*: you have to understand how they see things.
- *Defaults*: make sure the 'do nothing' route is one of the best.
- *Give feedback*: investigate the rejected options and experiment with them.
- *Expect error*: humans make mistakes, and well-designed systems allow for this.
- *Structure complex choices*: if it's difficult, break it down into easier chunks.

Any adept customer strategy needs to allow for all of this.

 SMART STRATEGY WARNING

Many strategies refer to customers as consumers, somehow imagining that they are all just waiting to lap up everything the brand has to offer and wolf it down for breakfast. This is condescending at best and commercially misleading at worst.

To avoid surprise, make sure that the means by which customers interact with the brand are well thought out, and allow for vagaries in behaviour as identified by behavioural economic theory.

7. SMALL CHANGES = BIG EFFECT

Persuasion science shows that, in today's information-overloaded world, it's often the smallest changes that can have the biggest influence.

Small changes can have a disproportionately big effect, according to Martin, Goldstein and Cialdini in *The Small Big*.

Their book contains over 50 deceptively simple suggestions and explains the scientific research behind them. There's nothing particularly devious about these – they are for anyone who wishes to change the behaviour of others effectively, efficiently *and* ethically.

In many cases, the alterations cost nothing but can, for example, save governments millions. Three simple yet powerful underlying human motivations provide the key to all of this. Most people want to:
* Make accurate decisions as efficiently as possible
* Affiliate with and gain the approval of others
* See themselves in a positive light.

Small changes are additionally powerful because they 'fly under the radar'. They rarely raise suspicion or attention, and simply go quietly about their business, so it can be easy to introduce them into a customer strategy without necessarily demanding large budgets.

For example, in 2009 the UK government was able to collect £200 million extra tax simply by truthfully stating on correspondence that "most UK citizens pay their tax on time".

This played to people's inherent desire to follow others and make an accurate decision as efficiently as possible.

Forget the big stuff for the moment, and consider the smallest change you could make that might have a significant effect.

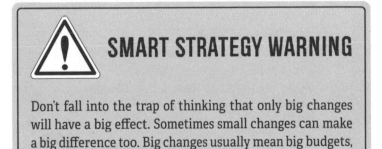

⚠ SMART STRATEGY WARNING

Don't fall into the trap of thinking that only big changes will have a big effect. Sometimes small changes can make a big difference too. Big changes usually mean big budgets, which are proportionally harder to secure.

Instead, forensically analyse the customer experience and work out all the small things that could be adjusted, often at a fraction of the cost.

SMART CUSTOMER STRATEGY SUMMARY

- Your research could be misleading you.
- Is there a thinking/doing gap?
- Are your customers really loyal?
- Are they really satisfied?
- Don't panic: service recovery can be beneficial.
- Customers make strange decisions.
- Small changes can have a disproportionately big effect.

A WORD ON SALES STRATEGY

In one or two exceptional cases, customer demand
is so high that a company barely has to make
an effort to sell its stuff.

This is extremely rare, so for everyone else a successful
selling approach is needed.

And that means an effective sales strategy.

But in some countries, notably the UK,
'sales' is a dirty word.

Even in the USA, the home of overt selling, people
spontaneously come up with words such as 'pushy', 'sleazy',
'annoying' and 'manipulative' to describe sales or selling.

But, in truth, we are all selling most of the time.

Want me to agree with you? Sell me your thought.

Want me to meet you at a certain place?
Sell me your proposed venue.

You get the idea.

Companies can no longer sell to people in a crass way.

Customers need to *want* to buy.

So, making a sale may be a complicated conversation
with many angles.

Let's have a look at how textured this can be.

PART FOUR

SALES
STRATEGY

1. SELLING ISN'T JUST FOR SALESPEOPLE

Selling is no longer solely the domain of salespeople, because we are all trying to move each other to our point of view in some way or another.

Good selling involves agitation rather than irritation. Identify the 1% question that's important, and the rest will fall into place, claims Daniel Pink in *To Sell Is Human*.

The old asymmetry, whereby the salesperson knew more than the customer, no longer applies. With a customer having conducted detailed research online, it may now be the other way around.

The way things are framed influences the likelihood of a sale.

Try offering less, labelling options differently, pointing out the pitfalls rather than just the benefits, explaining the potential, and offering an easy launch pad to get the purchase underway.

So, instead of *caveat emptor*, it is now a case of *caveat venditor* – seller beware.

The ABC of moving others is no longer 'always be closing'. It's now:

- *Attunement*: being in harmony with the potential customer and adopting their perspective.
- *Buoyancy*: grittiness of spirit and sunniness of outlook equal resilience.
- *Clarity*: finding problems and defining them to make sense of murky situations is as important as just solving them.

Interestingly, the best salespeople are neither extraverts nor introverts. They are 'ambiverts' – a bit of each. This is not a newly made-up word. It has been around since the 1920s.

Start by working out all of the customer interaction points in your company, and consider them as part of the sales process.

⚠ SMART STRATEGY WARNING

A sales strategy isn't just something to be handed to the sales department. The whole company needs to understand what the sales attitude is. And then every employee needs to enact it.

In many companies, the strategy is abrasive, overly pushy and entirely designed to generate numbers – whether that's new customers, cross-selling, increased frequency of purchase or higher margins. Pursuing numbers in their own right is a mistake. You need a philosophy first, with a suitable sales strategy to match.

2. SUCCESSFUL SELLING IS CHALLENGING

The best salespeople don't just build relations with customers – they challenge them.

According to Dixon and Adamson in their book *The Challenger Sale*, every sales rep in the world falls into one of five distinct profiles, and, while all can deliver average performance, only the 'challenger' delivers consistently high performance.

Based on their study of 6,000 sales reps, the five types are the hard worker, the challenger, the relationship builder, the lone wolf and the reactive problem solver.

Instead of leading with information about their company and its solutions, challengers provide customers with surprising insights about how they can save or make money.

They tailor their message to each customer, they are assertive (but not aggressive), and they push back where necessary to take control of the sale.

Challengers provided double the number of high performers in the study, and at least half of them were more likely to succeed in a high-complexity sales environment.

They have three main skills:
1. **Teaching for differentiation**: delivering insight that reframes the way customers think
2. **Tailoring for resonance**: communicating sales messages in the context of the customer
3. **Taking control of the sale**: openly pursuing goals in a direct but non-aggressive way to overcome increased customer risk aversion.

Sales strategies that have to deal with selling complicated products should bear all this in mind.

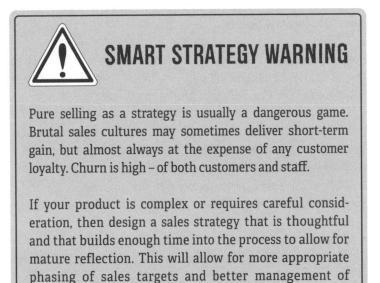

SMART STRATEGY WARNING

Pure selling as a strategy is usually a dangerous game. Brutal sales cultures may sometimes deliver short-term gain, but almost always at the expense of any customer loyalty. Churn is high – of both customers and staff.

If your product is complex or requires careful consideration, then design a sales strategy that is thoughtful and that builds enough time into the process to allow for mature reflection. This will allow for more appropriate phasing of sales targets and better management of expectation all round.

3. TRY RATIONAL DROWNING

Some sales strategies rely on a relentlessly cheerful approach. But in many contexts this is counter-productive.

In fact, it can pay to suggest that the issue is much harder than the potential customer believes.

Sometimes this involves taking the mood down for a short while to emphasize the severity of the problem. This is followed by bringing the customer back up with your proposed solution.

This is called 'rational drowning'. Effective commercial teaching usually involves six main stages:

1. **Warmer**: build credibility through empathy.
2. **Reframing**: shock the customer with the unknown.
3. **Rational drowning**: intensify the problem and then break it down.
4. **Emotional impact**: make the problem human.
5. **Value proposition**: introduce a new way, building confidence back up.
6. **Solution and implementation map**: describe in detail how to fix the problem with your product.

'Hypothesis-based selling' involves leading with a hypothesis of the customer's needs, informed by experience and research.

Bear in mind that having widespread support across an organization is now vital to likely sales success – going straight to the decision maker is unlikely to work.

KPMG has an interesting SAFE-BOLD framework that allows you to score from 1–10 the scale, risk, innovativeness and difficulty of any sales issue:
- SAFE = **S**mall, **A**chievable, **F**ollowing, **E**asy
- BOLD = **B**ig, **O**utperforming, **L**eading edge, **D**ifficult.

Interestingly, the sales experience contributes more to customer loyalty (53%) than the brand (19%), product and service delivery (19%), and value-to-price ratio (9%) put together, so it is really worth getting it right.

 SMART STRATEGY WARNING

Don't use rational drowning if the sales context is relatively simple. There's no need to frighten the horses if everything is pretty straightforward.

Bear in mind that many companies think that things are more complicated than they truly need to be. Many potential customers have a high level of understanding already, so it pays to understand how sophisticated your audience is and pitch your sales strategy accordingly.

4. THE HAMMOCK

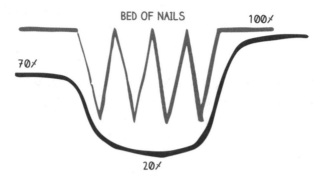

There are lots of ways to increase the chances of someone buying what you have to sell. If the sales process is reasonably complex, then your pitch must have a clear *point of view* and a decent *line of argument*.

Typically, this should involve:
1. **Grabber**: grab attention immediately with something unexpected.
2. **Pain**: show the prospect something that threatens their business.
3. **Impact**: identify the closeness and urgency of the problem.
4. **Contrast**: present a new way to look at the problem.
5. **Proof**: demonstrate how your proposal will work.

Grabbers that work well include number guessing games (put 10 million on a chart and ask the audience to guess what it refers to), customer stories with an emotional aspect, stating the opposite of what the prospect expects, and posing "What if you ...?" questions.

You'll notice that the word 'pain' equates to rational drowning. 'Provocation-based selling' delivers bad news and then fixes it.

Research shows that people remember 70% of the words at the beginning of a presentation, 20% in the middle, and 100% at the end. As a diagram, this pacing looks like a hammock.

Beware the bed of nails in the middle, where everyone gets bored.

Pace your pitch accordingly. You need some emotion, contrast, strong visuals, simplicity and proof, and you need to make it personal. Put your best points first and last.

Using diagrams creates *big pictures*. It's the best way to simplify a complex message and make abstract ideas concrete.

Start strongly, get out of the dip as quickly as possible, and end dramatically with a clear benefit.

⚠ SMART STRATEGY WARNING

Too many sales approaches involve droning on about the technical features of the product. These are only of limited interest and are often not the main point.

A thoughtful sales strategy will concentrate on the issues the customer faces and how the product or service can help to address them. Benefits are much stronger than features. Resist the temptation to waffle on about your stuff. Customers don't care how it works – they want to know how it helps them.

5. NEW BUSINESS COULD BE OLD BUSINESS

Some sales strategies are obsessed with *new* business.

They triumphantly (and often misleadingly) measure the numbers coming into the top of the sales funnel while failing to stem the flow of customers falling out of the leaky bucket.

This is not really a sales strategy.

Sales includes the maintenance of a healthy and satisfied customer base who are both happy to remain with your company and open to the idea of buying more from you when the time is right.

A classic example of getting this wrong is when brands make discounted offers to new customers that are clearly better than the terms their existing customers receive.

These are widely publicized so all existing customers can see, and they get grumpy as a result.

So a successful sales strategy will naturally include the need to *pitch*, but it must also be prepared to *improvise* and *serve* the customer.

The maths is interesting here too. It costs barely anything to retain a customer or sell them another product, but the cost of acquiring a new customer is always high.

Most sales strategies are too complicated.

Your first step should be to simplify everything.

The next step might be to try a *reverse pilot* – a notion we first came across in Part Two on brand strategy.

Test whether removing an initiative or activity will have any negative consequences. If not, take it out.

Remember: if it isn't a clear yes, then it's a clear no.

⚠ SMART STRATEGY WARNING

Be wary of setting macho targets for sales. Loading the pot with large amounts of new business may not be beneficial, particularly if existing customers are leaving in droves.

Make customer satisfaction a priority, thereby reducing the burden on brand new business. Then consider the complexity of the sales strategy and do everything possible to simplify it.

6. WEIRD IS THE NEW NORMAL

Let's face it – we're all weird. So says Seth Godin.

So why are companies still trying to sell products to the masses? Why are we still acting as though the masses even exist?

Mass is what allowed many businesses to become efficient. It's what we call the undifferentiated, the easily reached majority that seeks to conform.

Normal is what we call the people in the middle. But it is localized. What's normal here is not necessarily normal somewhere else.

Weird is what we call people who aren't normal. This means by choice, rather than unusual by nature or physique.

Rich refers to anyone who can make choices – who has enough resources to do more than merely survive.

Antelopes don't have hobbies. You need to be rich to be weird.

And a lot of products and services rely on brand cachet to justify premium pricing.

So there is a sales strategy here.

The bell curve is spreading. The bump of normal in the middle isn't gone, but it's much flatter, and flanked by many more weird outlying groups.

This can reward companies that create distinctive products for outliers, or those on the so-called long tail.

Fragmentation can lead to opportunity for many companies, if they identify and pursue the right type of more discerning customer.

 **SMART STRATEGY WARNING**

Don't try to sell everything to everyone. While it is tempting to chase large audiences to generate a higher sales number, it is often more beneficial to pursue fewer sales at a higher price or better margin.

Before arbitrarily decreeing a sales strategy with specific targets, have a look at the entire product mix. You may discover that having better products and services, justifying a higher price or margin to a more affluent customer base, is preferable.

7. THE STRATEGY/ EXECUTION GAP

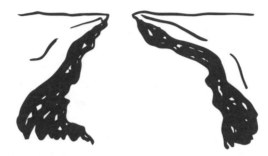

There's no point in having a brilliant sales strategy if it isn't executed effectively. Bridging the gap between strategy and execution is vital, a point elegantly made by Marty Neumeier in *The Brand Gap*.

In most companies, this is a chasm. There are left-brain strategists and marketing people on the one hand (analytical, logical, linear, concrete, numerical) and right-brain creative people on the other (intuitive, emotional, spatial, visual, physical).

This can cause a brilliant strategy to fail where it counts most – at the point of contact with the customer.

The gap can be bridged in five ways:
1. *Differentiate*: who are you, what do you do and why does it matter?
2. *Collaborate*: it's the survival of what Neumeier calls 'the fittingest'.
3. *Innovate*: design ignites passion, not strategy. Zag when others zig.
4. *Validate*: start a dialogue and pay proper attention to feedback.
5. *Cultivate*: looking after brands is never-ending.

So the successful company is not the one with the most brains but the one with the most brains acting in concert.

Turfismo is the behind-the-scenes politicking that ruins many initiatives.

Featuritis is an infectious desire for more that overloads products with far too much of everything.

In fact, the emphasis of customer appeal has shifted from features (what a product has) to benefits (what it does) to experience (what you'll feel) to identification (who you are).

Edward de Bono suggested that, instead of USP (unique selling proposition), brands should pay attention to UBS (the unique buying state of their customers).

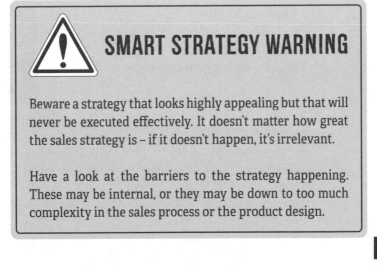

⚠ SMART STRATEGY WARNING

Beware a strategy that looks highly appealing but that will never be executed effectively. It doesn't matter how great the sales strategy is – if it doesn't happen, it's irrelevant.

Have a look at the barriers to the strategy happening. These may be internal, or they may be down to too much complexity in the sales process or the product design.

SMART SALES STRATEGY SUMMARY

- Selling isn't just for salespeople.
- Successful selling means challenging.
- Try rational drowning.
- Beware the hammock.
- New business could come from existing business.
- Weird is the new normal.
- Close the strategy/execution gap

A WORD ON PEOPLE STRATEGY

We talk of companies, corporations, boards and brands.

But they are all made up of people.

It has become fashionable to describe workforces variously
as human resources or human capital.

These descriptors have a strangely distancing effect.

We are, after all, still talking about people.

And people are very varied.

They can be viewed by job title, by department or as individuals.

Bosses can either be brilliant or ruin everything.

So can members of staff.

It's the interplay between the leaders and the rest that
holds the key to success or failure.

So we will look at people strategy from all angles: from the
overall company approach to how leaders should behave and
how individuals can perform to the best of their ability.

Drawing all of this together generates a people strategy
– one of the most important documents in any company.

PART FIVE

PEOPLE
STRATEGY

1. MANAGE THE PEOPLE, NOT THE NUMBERS

Effective leaders manage the people, not the numbers, according to Simon Sinek, which fits nicely with our 'pursue principles, not money' idea.

Proper leaders are the ones who put their interests aside for the greater good. They would sooner sacrifice what is theirs to save what is ours.

This makes followers feel safe (a primal need), which is why they will work tirelessly to see their leaders' visions come to life.

In a circle of safety, we feel like we belong.

In the US Marines at mealtimes, the junior people are served first. This reinforces the fact that the true price of leadership is the willingness to place the needs of others above your own.

Leaders eat last.

To cope, they need to:
• Bring people together and keep it real
• Keep the numbers manageable
• Meet their staff properly
• Give their staff time (not just money)
• Be patient in waiting for results.

In strong organizations, people break the rules because it is the right thing to do for others.

In weak organizations, people break the rules for personal gain.

The Boomer generation is described as the *pig in the python* – a demographic bulge that grew up used to getting what it wanted.

When these people became leaders, they had a negative effect on what proper leadership should be, which is why we now have so many leadership failures.

Look after the people and the numbers will follow.

⚠ SMART STRATEGY WARNING

If you want people to follow you, don't set a number as an objective. A number is not a vision, mission or goal, and it's not motivating.

Creating vicious tension in a company may create short-term value, but it also causes deep resentment. At General Electric, Jack Welch introduced a 'rank and yank' policy. Every year he would fire the bottom-performing 10% of managers and reward the top 20% with stock options. Nice bloke. Avoid such banality.

2. CLEAR THINKING + COURAGEOUS ACTION

To make the best decisions, leaders need a blend of clear, detached thinking and courage to take action, according to Phil Rosenzweig in his book *Left Brain, Right Stuff*.

Your *left brain* has a talent for clear analysis. That's logic.

The *right stuff* is the willingness to take bold action. That's bravery.

Making decent decisions depends on the questions you ask first. The best ones are:

- ***Are we making a decision about something we cannot control, or are we able to influence outcomes?*** If you can't, don't bother. Equally, many managers underestimate the effect they can have, which can be just as bad.
- ***Are we seeking an absolute level of performance, or is performance relative?*** Are we trying to do well or to do better than our rivals? Constantly looking at the competition can be irrelevant, but aiming both to exert control *and* outperform rivals is the hardest thing.

- ***Are we making a decision that lends itself to rapid feedback, so we can make adjustments and improve our next effort?*** If not, think harder to reduce error. If it takes a year to find out, it may be too late.
- ***Are we clear about what we mean by 'overconfidence'?*** The term is usually used in hindsight, but some level of confidence or bravery is certainly necessary, otherwise too many managers will believe they are powerless.
- ***When the course of action is uncertain, do we have a sense of the side on which we should err?*** Sometimes doing nothing is preferable, but not if it consistently leads to a mood of helplessness.

Answering these questions candidly will ensure that people really do know what they are doing and can adjust appropriately to changing circumstances.

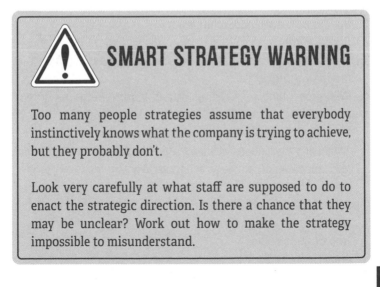

⚠ SMART STRATEGY WARNING

Too many people strategies assume that everybody instinctively knows what the company is trying to achieve, but they probably don't.

Look very carefully at what staff are supposed to do to enact the strategic direction. Is there a chance that they may be unclear? Work out how to make the strategy impossible to misunderstand.

3. ENSURE ORGANIZATIONAL HEALTH

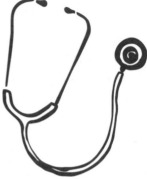

Patrick Lencioni believes that organizational health is more important than everything else.

Companies look to the same old stuff to gain a competitive advantage, but the untapped goldmine they often fail to exploit is making sure that the people in the business work properly. The four components of this are:

1. Build a cohesive leadership team.
2. Create clarity.
3. Over-communicate clarity – CEOs really need to be 'chief reminding officers'.
4. Reinforce clarity – 'starting true rumours' helps to spread information effectively.

The leadership team needs to build *trust*, allow for and master *conflict*, achieve *commitment*, embrace *accountability* and focus on *results*.

There are six critical questions that need to be answered to create clarity:

1. Why do we exist?
2. How do we behave?
3. What do we do?

4. How will we succeed?
5. What is most important, right now?
6. Who must do what?

Once these have been properly answered, they need to be repeated again and again to staff, and reinforced with appropriate behaviour.

A *thematic goal* is a rallying cry designed to defeat silos, politics and turf wars. It needs to be singular, qualitative and temporary, so that everyone in the company knows what to do *right now*.

Good communication arises from avoiding *meeting stew*. Try having just four types of meeting:
1. Daily check-in (10 minutes)
2. Weekly staff (45–90 minutes)
3. Ad hoc topical (2–4 hours)
4. Quarterly offsite (1–2 days).

Amazingly, these will only take up 13% of your time.

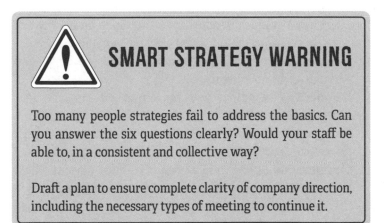

⚠ SMART STRATEGY WARNING

Too many people strategies fail to address the basics. Can you answer the six questions clearly? Would your staff be able to, in a consistent and collective way?

Draft a plan to ensure complete clarity of company direction, including the necessary types of meeting to continue it.

4. GET PEOPLE IN FLOW

In his classic work on how to achieve happiness, called *Flow*, the near-unpronounceable Drucker School of Management professor Mihaly Csikszentmihalyi was the first to articulate the concept of 'flow'. (His name is actually pronounced 'cheeks-sent-me-high', and everyone calls him Mike apparently.)

This is the state in which people are so involved in an activity that nothing else seems to matter. It has eight major components:

1. ***A challenging activity that requires skills***: we must have a chance of completing it.
2. ***The merging of action and awareness***: we must be able to concentrate.
3. ***Clear goals***: we need to be clear about what we are doing ...
4. ***Immediate feedback***: ... and see immediate progress.
5. ***Concentration on the task at hand***: we must have effortless involvement removed from everyday worries and frustrations.
6. ***The paradox of control***: there must be a sense of control, even if you are not quite sure how you are achieving it.

7. **The loss of self-consciousness**: concern for the self disappears, but the person emerges stronger after the experience.
8. **The transformation of time**: hours can pass by in minutes, or minutes can stretch out to seem like hours.

This leads to an *autotelic experience* (from *auto* meaning 'self' and *telos* meaning 'goal') – a self-contained activity in which the doing of it is the reward in itself. The 'autotelic self' is a happy person. They can:
1. **Set goals**: have something to strive for
2. **Become immersed in the activity**: get lost in it
3. **Pay attention to what is happening**: be present in the here and now
4. **Learn to enjoy the immediate experience**: rather than crave something else.

Now that's a truly engaged employee.

⚠ SMART STRATEGY WARNING

Most companies have working space that actively prevents flow. An intelligent people strategy will try to work out how to allow as many staff as possible to be in flow so that they can produce their best work.

This means arranging a suitable environment in which to work and a system involving minimal interruption – something that most modern companies with open-plan offices completely fail to do.

5. TRUST AND TEAMWORK

According to Patrick Lencioni, five dysfunctions can ruin the effectiveness and cohesion of any leadership team:

1. **Absence of trust**: this stems from an unwillingness to be vulnerable within the group. Those who are not open about mistakes and weaknesses make it impossible to build trust.

2. **Fear of conflict**: teams that lack trust are incapable of engaging in unfiltered debate.

3. **Lack of commitment**: without having aired their opinions openly, team members rarely commit to decisions, though they may feign doing so.

4. **Avoidance of accountability**: without committing to a clear plan of action, even the most focused people fail to call their peers on counterproductive behaviour.

5. **Inattention to results**: failure to hold one another accountable creates an environment where team members put their individual or departmental needs above those of the team.

In fact, teams at all levels can fall prey to these deficiencies. Viewed from a more positive perspective, though, there are three essential virtues that make someone the ideal team player, at board or any other level:

- **Humble**: humility is the greatest and most indispensable attribute.

- **_Hungry_**: these people are self-motivated and diligent.
- **_Smart_**: these people demonstrate common sense when dealing with others (this is not the same as intellectual smartness).

Those with just one characteristic are fairly easy to spot:
- **_Humble only_**: the pawn, who often gets left out.
- **_Hungry only_**: the bulldozer, who often annoys everyone else.
- **_Smart only_**: the charmer, with great social skills but low contribution.

Those with two out of three are much harder to identify:
- **_Humble and hungry_**: the accidental mess-maker, unaware of their effect on people.
- **_Humble and smart_**: the lovable slacker, who only does as much as asked.
- **_Hungry and smart_**: the skilful politician, out for their own benefit.

> ⚠️ **SMART STRATEGY WARNING**
>
> There is far too much passive resistance in teams. Just because people don't say they disagree, it doesn't mean that they agree. An effective people strategy needs to address two fundamental points.
>
> 1. Do the members of the leadership team debate robustly, trust each other, commit to action and hold each other accountable?
> 2. What are the characteristics of team members and are they complementary?

6. EVERYONE CAN MASTER SOMETHING

Author Robert Greene believes that everyone has the potential to master something if they identify their true calling, patiently serve their apprenticeship and put in enough effort.

Mastery of a subject or skill is not down to luck or having innate skill. Anyone can achieve it with the right approach. It is attained through three stages: apprenticeship, the creative-active phase and then eventual mastery.

The apprenticeship phase involves deep observation, skills acquisition and lots of experimentation – moving from passive to practice to active mode. True apprentices value learning over money, keep expanding their horizons, move towards resistance and pain, and advance through trial and error.

The *mentor dynamic* is important – masters choose their mentors according to needs and inclinations, transfigure their ideas and create a back-and-forth dynamic that inspires them.

Seven deadly realities are the enemies of mastery: envy, conformism, rigidity, self-obsession, laziness, flightiness and passive aggression.

People strategies need to work hard to combat these traits around the company.

Nothing gets done if no one can be bothered. And this means that motivation has to be effective, with everybody working at a consistently high level. That's easier said than done.

In his book *Drive*, Daniel Pink boils the essence of motivation down to three crucial elements:
- *Autonomy* is the desire to direct our own lives.
- *Mastery* is the urge to get better and better at something that matters.
- *Purpose* is the yearning to do what we do in the service of something larger than ourselves.

People strategies need to create the environment in which these qualities can flourish.

⚠ SMART STRATEGY WARNING

People need to be provided with the right conditions to do their best work. Bosses and processes must allow people to do their stuff unencumbered. How many of the seven deadly realties are prevalent in your company?

A smart people strategy should examine every aspect of who does what and how they get things done, and, if needed, re-engineer everything so that it works better.

7. THE POWER OF CLEVERS

Smart, creative staff hold the key to company success, according to authors Rob Goffee and Gareth Jones.

Research shows that a handful of star performers create disproportionate amounts of value for their organizations. They aren't free agents who do this on their own – they need their organization's commercial and financial resources to fulfil their potential.

These invaluable individuals are called 'clevers' – they can be brilliant, difficult and sometimes even dangerous, and success may well depend on how well they are led, which is a nightmare in itself. Traditional leadership approaches won't be effective, so you need a particularly astute approach to leading these smart, creative people.

Bosses need to:
- Tell them what to do – not how to do it
- Earn their respect with expertise – not a job title
- Provide 'organized space' for their creativity
- Sense their needs and keep them motivated
- Shelter them from administrative and political distractions ('organizational rain')
- Connect them with clever peers
- Convince them that the company can help them succeed.

Their characteristics are:
- Their cleverness is central to their identity

- Their skills are not easily replicated
- They know their worth
- They ask difficult questions
- They are organizationally savvy
- They are not impressed by hierarchy
- They expect instant success
- They want to be connected to other clever people
- They won't thank you.

On top of these, they have a number of bad characteristics:
- Taking pleasure in breaking the rules
- Trivializing the importance of non-technical people
- Being oversensitive about their projects
- Suffering from knowledge-is-power syndrome
- Never being happy about the review process.

They can be hard to deal with, but the good news is that clevers attract more clevers.

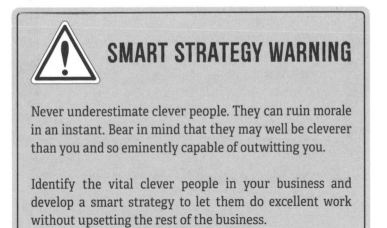

⚠ SMART STRATEGY WARNING

Never underestimate clever people. They can ruin morale in an instant. Bear in mind that they may well be cleverer than you and so eminently capable of outwitting you.

Identify the vital clever people in your business and develop a smart strategy to let them do excellent work without upsetting the rest of the business.

SMART PEOPLE STRATEGY SUMMARY

- Manage the people, not the numbers.
- Think clearly, then act courageously.
- Ensure organizational health.
- Get people in flow.
- Foster trust and teamwork.
- Everyone can master something.
- Harness the power of clevers.

A WORD ON INNOVATION STRATEGY

Innovation is one of the most overused words in business.

It is usually uttered by dismayed executives who realize that nothing interesting is being suggested.

Innovation is really just a lazy euphemism for anyone having a decent idea.

The purpose of an innovation strategy is to create the conditions in which smart new ideas can be generated in an orderly fashion.

In other words, it doesn't work if random ideas are popping up all over the place all year.

There needs to be a systematic approach, so that ideas are harnessed in a manageable way, ensuring that the right number of excellent initiatives are dreamed up and enacted effectively.

You will often see it said that innovation is the lifeblood of successful business.

That's not strictly true.

It is possible to do straightforward things well and consistently – with a few updates.

An analysis of nearly 18 million scientific papers discovered that 90% of what was in these apparently 'creative' manuscripts was actually old stuff recycled.

So innovation is effectively 90% known material with a 10% interesting twist provided by new developments or perspectives.

PART SIX

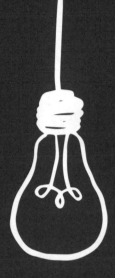

INNOVATION STRATEGY

1. THE CREATIVITY + COMMERCE CROSSROADS

Innovation must build ideas at the crossroads of creativity and commerce, according to Mark Payne, founder of the innovation company Fahrenheit 212.

The failure rates of most innovations are absurdly high, culminating in *unicorns* – visions that are lovely to think about but only doable and profitable in some imaginary world.

What is needed is a *money and magic* approach, sometimes called *how and wow*.

That's where the ideas people *and* the commercial people work together from the off to solve both a big customer problem and a big business problem in one bold move.

What goes into an innovation process is always dozens of initiatives competing for resources.

By the midpoint, nearly all solve a customer need. But they should only be implemented if they also solve a business need for the company.

The moral is: don't suspend commercial questions early in the process.

This two-sided thinking (customer need and company need) must be present from day one, because the best results appear at the crossroads of these two requirements.

Another crossroads comes at the intersection of near-term ROI (return on investment), low risk tolerance, big growth goals and tight resource constraints.

Big doesn't always have to mean risky, slow and expensive.

So don't buy into the myth that creativity is most effective when it's unencumbered by practical imperatives. That's not true.

⚠ SMART STRATEGY WARNING

Creativity in isolation does not form the basis of a decent innovation strategy. It has to be applied to a true commercial need. So having random ideas without understanding the real commercial issues doesn't get you anywhere.

For a truly effective innovation approach, get the practical people working at the beginning with the ideas people. This will save you generating scores of idealistic concepts that can't be executed. We will develop this idea more next.

2. SIT AND AUDIT

For a truly effective innovation strategy, try using what Goldenberg and Boyd call *Systematic Inventive Thinking* (SIT). This involves:

- **Subtraction**: list the product's main components; remove one essential component, partially or fully; visualize the result (no matter how strange); consider the potential benefits or new markets for the new version.
- **Division**: list the components; divide the product functionally or physically; visualize the new version; look for benefits and markets.
- **Multiplication**: list the components; make copies of a component; change one of the essential attributes of the copy; visualize and look for benefits.
- **Task unification**: give a component an additional task, either internal or external; look for new benefits.

The benefits of this approach can be huge. Subtracting can make products and services so much simpler.

Division can do so as well and can lead to new products with different purposes.

Multiplication and unification can lead to variety or to multipurpose products or services.

Another helpful approach is to conduct a beliefs audit:
- What are the inherent assumptions in your day-to-day work?
- What has your organization never feared that could destroy it?
- If your company didn't exist, what difference would it make?

These are penetrating questions that challenge the norm and can lead to fresh thinking.

It pays to SIT and audit what is currently happening.

Doing so could certainly lead to an interesting innovation.

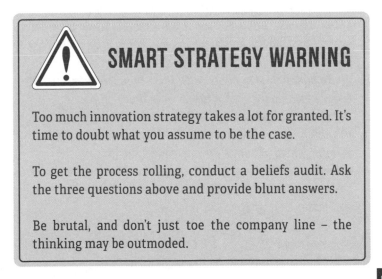

⚠ SMART STRATEGY WARNING

Too much innovation strategy takes a lot for granted. It's time to doubt what you assume to be the case.

To get the process rolling, conduct a beliefs audit. Ask the three questions above and provide blunt answers.

Be brutal, and don't just toe the company line – the thinking may be outmoded.

3. SEE YOUR BUSINESS AS A SERVICE

Viewing your business as a service rather than just a product adds a whole extra dimension to it. So said Henry Chesbrough, the originator of the idea of open innovation.

Four concepts and practices are crucial to getting this done:

1. **Think of your business as a service business** in order to sustain profitability and achieve new growth, regardless of your current view.
2. **Invite customers to contribute their ideas** to generate better experiences, so they get more of what they really want.
3. **Being open accelerates service innovation**, resulting in more choice for customers and a platform for others to build on, and allowing you to generate new revenue streams.
4. **Effective service innovation transforms business models** to create profit from internal initiatives, stimulate external ones, and add overall value to the business.

Many companies stagnate by concentrating solely on product, something often referred to as the commodity trap.

Manufacturing and business knowledge and insights are now widely distributed, and product manufacturing has moved to areas of the world with very low costs.

So there is a shrinking amount of time that a product can last before a new and improved one takes its place.

Continuing to run on this treadmill will not lead to growth.

Open innovation assumes that firms can and should use external ideas as well as internal ones.

This can even mean that their competitors move from being threatening leaders to happy followers or even collaborators.

SMART STRATEGY WARNING

Too many companies simply produce products. In fact, they should be solving some kind of customer need by serving them in some way.

So the key to an effective innovation strategy is to provide these services – not just to make stuff that the company feels comfortable doing. So, even if you do not believe you are in a service industry, ask yourself this question: How can your company innovate what it does to provide a better service?

4. MAKE YOUR OWN LUCK

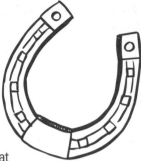

Innovation expert Scott D. Anthony says that any company has the ability to innovate.

He defines innovation as "something different that has impact".

The seven deadly sins of innovation are:
1. *Pride*: forcing your view of quality onto the market
2. *Sloth*: allowing innovation efforts to slow to a crawl
3. *Gluttony*: throwing too much resource at something
4. *Lust*: getting distracted chasing too many bright, shiny objects
5. *Envy*: pitting the core business against innovation efforts
6. *Wrath*: punishing risk takers severely
7. *Greed*: being impatient for growth, leading to the pursuit of low-potential markets.

Matt Kingdon, founder of innovation company ?What If!, says that a lot of innovation in big business appears to be a happy accident, but in truth good innovators make their own luck by forcing connections, trying things out and never giving up.

This is the 'science of serendipity', which takes determination, provocation, experimentation and political savvy. Its components are:
- *The protagonist*: 'captain one minute, pirate the next'. Someone has to be the catalyst if you want to get anything done.

This person must use an unusual blend of ambition, humility, confidence and flexibility, as well as being a finisher.

- **The quest for provocation**: this means deliberately managing inspiration by getting out of the office and finding proper insights.
- **Making ideas real**: this involves translating ideas into a form that people can react to immediately and emotionally – usually a working prototype of some kind.
- **Collision course**: this entails using the physical environment to create space for serendipity. Conventional offices don't foster innovation – you need messy areas where people can collide.
- **Battling the corporate machine**: navigating naysayers and inevitable roadblocks is arguably the hardest bit.

You really can make your own luck.

⚠ SMART STRATEGY WARNING

Many companies write down aspirational stuff but don't change anything to help those ambitions occur. If innovation is to succeed, it requires the right conditions.

Analyse your company and ask penetrating questions. Who are your protagonists? Are people encouraged to leave the office for more interesting stimuli? Where can people produce prototypes? What part of the machine blocks innovation?

5. COMPETE ON ALL FRONTS AT ONCE

Here's an odd piece of advice: do everything at once.

Larry Downes and Paul Nunes, from the Accenture Institute for High Performance, argue that successful innovation means you should compete on all fronts at the same time, market to everyone immediately, and constantly recombine the efforts of low-cost experiments to create improved products.

Conventional wisdom suggests you focus on just one discipline, target a small group of early adopters and eventually innovate to meet the needs of underserved segments. Downes and Nunes recommend the opposite.

It used to take years for new products and services to dethrone industry leaders. Now any business can be instantly devastated by something better and cheaper.

Start-ups can unravel your strategy before you even begin to grasp what's happening, and they may not even see you as competition – you could simply be collateral damage.

The Rogers bell curve of innovators, early adopters, early and late majorities, and laggards is now out of date. It has been replaced by a steep shark's fin of trial users and everyone else. This has four components:

1. *The singularity*: an early and long flat phase punctuated by a few market experiments
2. *The big bang*: in which a new product or service totally disrupts the old order, very quickly
3. *The big crunch*: where the disruptor enters a mature state and things unravel
4. *Entropy*: the last phase of a dying industry (the last elements may recombine to generate the next singularity).

 SMART STRATEGY WARNING

Does your innovation strategy put all your eggs in one basket? Could you create an alternative in which you launch a wider series of experiments?

Many companies simply wish to replicate high-volume cash cows that are similar to what they already have. But what about getting in and out quickly? Could you design an innovation strategy in which you shed your assets before they become liabilities? Could you then quit while you are ahead?

6. THE FRAUGHT FIRST MILE

Scott D. Anthony reckons that the 'first mile' is where an idea moves from existing on paper to existing in a market. This stage is the one most commonly afflicted with failure. It's where danger lurks.

Less than 1% of ideas launched by big companies end up working.

The ideas aren't the problem – it's the process. Anthony proposes one called DEFT:

- **Document**: write down the answers to these questions: is there a need, can we deliver, do the numbers work and does it matter?
- **Evaluate**: look at things from multiple perspectives and determine what the unknowns are.
- **Focus**: work out the deal killers and path dependencies (uncertainties that affect subsequent strategic choices).
- **Test**: learn and adjust, use small teams, design tests carefully and savour surprises.

Fill out the '4P model': population, purchase frequency, price per transaction and penetration. This quick piece of maths gives a feel for likely success.

Our confidence in new projects is usually overstated because we overestimate our ability to control events and are over-confident in assessing outcomes with wide ranges. Meanwhile, we underestimate risks and ignore black swan events.

Long-winded and time-consuming business plans are a waste of time. Instead, innovators should spend just enough time capturing the essence of their idea so they can get on with it.

The *spreadsheet dance* is also a waste of time. This is when the innovation team draws up a revenue projection for the new venture, only to be told to increase the numbers. The 'minimum acceptable answer' needs careful scrutiny. And many innovations are impossible to forecast.

As statistician George Box said, "All models are wrong but some are useful."

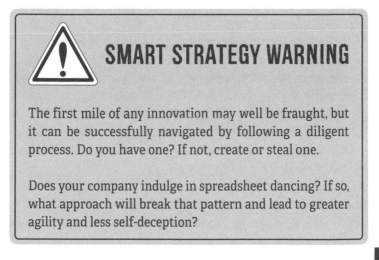

⚠ SMART STRATEGY WARNING

The first mile of any innovation may well be fraught, but it can be successfully navigated by following a diligent process. Do you have one? If not, create or steal one.

Does your company indulge in spreadsheet dancing? If so, what approach will break that pattern and lead to greater agility and less self-deception?

7. KEEP IT FRUGAL

If all else fails, there are plenty of intelligent ways to do a lot with very little. Navi Radjou and Jaideep Prabhu call this frugal innovation, and they reckon it is the future.

Frugal innovation is all about how to do more with less: faster, cheaper, better. It allows companies to get high-quality products to market quickly using limited resources.

They propose six principles:
1. **Engage and iterate**: the research and development function of large companies must focus on the customer.
2. **Flex your assets**: companies can save money, resources and time by making better use of what they have: production, distribution and services.
3. **Create sustainable solutions**: cradle to cradle needs to replace lab to landfill (the perpetual recycling of products rather than just throwing them away).
4. **Share customer behaviour**: all of this is irrelevant unless companies get people to change their behaviour.
5. **Co-create value with customers**: they can help to identify new ideas, validate them, and develop them into products or services.

6. ***Make innovative friends***: keeping industrial secrets no longer
   works – look for partnerships to solve tricky problems.

Businesses need to open up, moving from 'not invented here' to 'proudly found elsewhere'.

Big business can learn from start-ups: keep things simple, work quickly, find solutions through multiple partnerships and don't be afraid of uncertainty.

Vertically integrated supply chains controlled by companies should now be replaced with a horizontal economy: the maker movement of tinkerers and peer-to-peer sharing platforms.

DIY should be replaced with DIWO – do it with others.

 SMART STRATEGY WARNING

Innovation strategy doesn't have to involve vast expense. It is more a state of mind – allowing for experimentation in a non-threatening environment in which it is okay to make mistakes and learn.

Is this an approach that could work for your company? Does something about the current innovation approach need to change? What help from outside might be needed to make that happen?

SMART INNOVATION STRATEGY SUMMARY

- Work at the crossroads between creativity and commerce.
- SIT and audit.
- See your business as a service.
- Make your own luck.
- Compete on all fronts at once.
- Overcome the fraught first mile.
- Keep it frugal.

A WORD ON
COMMUNICATION STRATEGY

Finally, after all this good thinking has been done and direction agreed, it needs to be conveyed to everyone who needs to know.

And that means a well-considered communication strategy.

There is nothing in the world that cannot be misunderstood.

A communication strategy might intend one thing and unintentionally convey another.

You can't be clear enough.

So make sure your work isn't riddled with opaque language that seems to say something but that actually confuses everyone.

A strategy itself has to communicate, regardless of topic.

So a communication strategy has a double responsibility: to be understood in its own right and to make something else understood.

You'll see therefore that, somewhat strangely, a communication strategy may well even require its own communication strategy.

All of this adds up to quite a heavy burden.

Over £21 billion was spent on advertising in the UK in 2016. Only 13% of it was even noticed, and 7% was disliked.

Something isn't working, so let's make it better.

PART SEVEN

COMMUNICATION STRATEGY

1. SAY LESS FOR MORE IMPACT

You can make a bigger impact by saying less. According to Joseph McCormack in his book *Brief*, most day-to-day communications are unfocused and unclear.

In a world where everyone is inundated with too much information and highly inattentive, being brief isn't a nicety, it's a necessity.

People who struggle with brevity suffer variously from any or all of the seven Cs: cowardice, (over)confidence, callousness, comfort, confusion, complication and carelessness.

Audiences of all types that are 'mind-filled' rather than 'mindful' suffer from inundation, inattention, interruption and impatience.

There are four things you need to do to communicate effectively and efficiently:

1. *Map it*: map out the argument, then condense and trim volumes of information from it.
2. *Tell it*: use narrative storytelling to explain the message in a clear, concise and compelling way.
3. *Talk it*: McCormack's TALC system turns monologues in meetings into controlled, productive conversations: talk, actively listen, converse.

4. **Show it**: use visuals to attract attention and capture the imagination.

Brevity is not just about time. It doesn't just mean being concise.
- **Light brevity** is being concise without comprehension.
- **Deep brevity** is being succinct with savvy. Aim for this.

Pretty much every strategy is sold to colleagues and bosses in presentations. All strategic presentations should be subject to trimming. McCormack identifies three levels of information that can make a persuasive case:
- **Level 1** details are absolutely essential.
- **Level 2** details add a little flavour but shouldn't take up too much time.
- **Level 3** items weigh the story down and don't make it noticeably better.

 SMART STRATEGY WARNING

Is your strategy too long-winded? Long doesn't equal interesting. In fact, it probably means vague and confusing. Do you have too many level 3 points?

Take your strategy, grab some sticky notes and write down only one strong point per note – the fewer the better. Then spend a little time putting these points in a persuasive order. Remember: if your colleagues don't understand it, then your audience has no chance.

2. POLITE DIRECTNESS

There are many ways to communicate. Combining directness with politeness is probably the best combination.

But a range of studies show that cultures differ hugely on how material is presented.

For example, in the USA, 'bottom line upfront' is usually the best way to start any presentation. Your message will immediately be clear and will remain so even if the meeting is cut short or someone has to leave early.

But the Germans may not like that. They may well think: how can you tell me your conclusions when we haven't discussed the details yet?

And the French won't necessarily agree separate points in a sequential agenda one at a time. They will see everything as connected and may not make a decision on item one until they have debated the rest.

And so on around the world. Richard Lewis's book *When Cultures Collide* explains many of these differences.

As James Bannerman points out, audience character types also vary. They may include those keen on:

- **Results**: Don't bore me with details. Make snappy points. Talk results.
- **Emotions**: Show genuine interest in my feelings. Give me help and support.
- **Abracadabra**: Give it some magic. Make it interesting and sparky.
- **Data**: Make research, facts and figures perfectly precise.

You need to be part psychologist and be able to READ your audience.

WIFM stands for **W**hat's **I**n **I**t **F**or **M**e?'. All presenters should consider this question in relation to the people to whom they are presenting.

Know what motivates your audience, skip what doesn't matter and make a conclusive delivery.

Flagging is calling out the number of ideas you want to share. This provides an order to any presentation and keeps the audience connected, waiting for you to deliver that number of points.

 SMART STRATEGY WARNING

Don't write a one-size-fits-all strategy or strategic presentation. If you want to communicate effectively, you need to think hard about the nature of the people with whom you are communicating.

Spend time working out the most likely style that will make them agree with you, and do this before you start writing anything down.

3. GIVE IT SOCIAL CURRENCY

So let's assume that your colleagues, bosses or clients have agreed to the strategy. How will you get your audience to understand it and like it?

Your message is more likely to catch on if you give it what author Jonah Berger calls 'social currency', or make it 'contagious'. This requires:

- **Social currency:** the message needs to make people look intelligent if they pass it on. We share things that make us look good. Can you find something that makes people feel like insiders?
- **Triggers**: provide related stimuli to remind people to talk about the message. Top of mind leads to tip of tongue. What cues can make people think about your product or idea?
- **Emotion**: when we care, we share. Ideas need to make people feel something. Concentrate on feelings: how can you kindle the fire and get people talking about it?

- **Public**: we need to see other people joining in. If it's built to show, it's built to grow. Can people see others using your product, or is there evidence that sticks around when they have?
- **Practical value**: it needs to be useful, according to the principle of 'news you can use'. Does the subject matter help people to help others?
- **Stories**: these increase appeal and help to engage people – information often travels under the guise of idle chatter. Is your product part of a broader story that people want to share?

Follow these components and your idea is more likely to go viral or lead to 'social transmission'.

⚠️ SMART STRATEGY WARNING

It's the old problem: just because you follow some appropriate steps, it doesn't mean that everyone is going to love what you communicate. But you can work out the sequence in advance, anticipate the sticking points, and build your strategy appropriately.

Whatever you do, don't convince yourself that everyone will be thrilled to engage with your communication and pass it on enthusiastically. They probably won't, unless you have really worked out their motivations beforehand.

4. DISADVANTAGE CAN BE ADVANTAGE

A lot of people in business bemoan the fact that they could have a grandiose communication strategy if they had more resources. This is nonsense.

Being at an apparent disadvantage can actually be an advantage.

In his book *David and Goliath*, Malcolm Gladwell points out that underdogs frequently develop hidden talents to gain an advantage. They are often tougher and more ingenious than those supposedly with more power.

So a degree of misfortune can be a tremendous asset – something Gladwell calls *desirable difficulty* or *relative deprivation*.

It's all about turning apparent constraints into sources of possibility and advantage. Contrary to popular belief, constraints can lead to more originality and ingenuity.

If you feel strategically limited, work through these stages recommended by Morgan and Barden in *A Beautiful Constraint*:
- ***Get out of the victim stage***: "We're really inhibited here."

- ***Move through the neutralizing stage***: "Our ambition is too important to allow this constraint to inhibit it."
- ***Arrive at the transformer stage***: "Let's use this to stimulate better thinking."
- ***Break path dependence***: most companies have processes, assumptions and ways of thinking that define "the way we do things round here". This locked-in path is predictable and often doesn't work.

A final approach is *Can If*. This comes mainly from Colin Kelly, Director of Research & Development at Warburtons. Instead of listening to naysayers saying "We can't, because", he insists on problem-solving language re-phrased as *"We can if"*.

This approach keeps optimism in the process and forces people to take responsibility for finding answers, rather than merely identifying barriers.

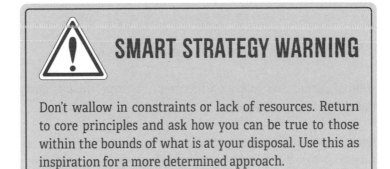

⚠ SMART STRATEGY WARNING

Don't wallow in constraints or lack of resources. Return to core principles and ask how you can be true to those within the bounds of what is at your disposal. Use this as inspiration for a more determined approach.

Instead of saying "We can't, because", start with "We can if". Look widely and impartially at these possibilities and work hard at ways to make them reality.

5. DO THINGS AND TELL PEOPLE

Media commentator Faris Yakob recommends that brands should do things and tell people, working with their customer community to recombine ideas constantly.

That's the opposite of telling people things when you haven't necessarily done them. In other words, avoid baseless communication at all costs.

If it isn't true, then don't claim it, and certainly don't communicate it. This sounds self-evident, but brands do it all the time.

Communication is persuasion, but attention is like water.

Without getting too heavy on this topic, brands are effectively socially constructed ideas.

Brand experiences build 'brandgrams' in our heads. In his book *Paid Attention*, Yakob explains that this is based on psychologist Daniel Schacter's belief that memories are encoded in the brain as engrams.

These are neuron-firing patterns that create a hypothetical permanent change in the brain that accounts for the existence of memory.

Brands can therefore become behavioural templates.

So an effective communication strategy needs to package ideas to attract the most attention and provide a robust model for influencing human behaviour.

Customer service is a form of marketing. And technology is a medium. But the medium isn't the message any more, because the difference between content, media and advertising is vanishing.

Do things and tell people: that's how to behave in a world of infinite content.

SMART STRATEGY WARNING

This one is complicated, but no one said communication strategy was easy. Start by analysing how tangible your brand is. The more intangible it is, the harder effective communication may be.

Plot how opinions of the brand might appear in the mind of the customer but, whatever you do, do not overstate the importance of the brand in their lives. Most marketers have far too high an opinion of their own brands, whereas most customers simply don't have the time to think about them.

Now consider the most powerful way to link your brand to customer thought and, ultimately, their behaviour.

6. MIND YOUR LANGUAGE

Anyone who wishes to communicate effectively needs to think carefully about the language they use.

This applies whether you are a senior leader of a company or simply trying to explain your communication strategy.

In a somewhat ironic twist, you will invariably need a communication strategy to explain your communication strategy.

So, if your strategy is full of clichés, bullshit and the same old language we always see, it won't be impressive.

Equally, leaders who don't rehearse and think they can "riff off some slides", even when they haven't even seen them before, set a very bad example.

In his book *The Language of Leaders*, Kevin Murray says that inspiring communication is vital, and he offers some help. Among the ideas that are relevant here are:
- Create a clear and vivid view of the future, and tell everybody.
- Engage and align people through conversations.
- Listen hard to inspire – be interested, respectful and patient.
- Stand up to stand out – you need a point of view.
- Use stories and anecdotes to motivate people.

- Don't send out signals that undermine your words.
- Prepare properly for public platforms – your reputation is at stake.
- Learn, rehearse, review and improve – always try to get better.

These are wise words for gaining agreement to any communication strategy, and indeed for enacting one effectively.

One final point: whatever you say, keep it as short as possible.

TLDR stands for "Too long, didn't read". TLDW stands for "Too long, didn't watch".

Make sure your material doesn't fall into these categories.

 SMART STRATEGY WARNING

Review any draft version you have of your communication strategy. Now begin work on a communication strategy for the communication strategy. Unless people agree with you, it's just so many words on what is probably a lot of paper.

Highlight all of the same old words and phrases you have seen before and replace them with more interesting language.

7. LEARN FROM MISTAKES

We know that a huge proportion of marketing and communication effort is completely wasted.

So it pays to review the most common mistakes that marketers and communications practitioners make, and there are lots of them.

Here are just a few highlighted by authors Hofmeyr and Rice:

- *Trying to have a relationship with customers who don't want one*: lots of customers simply don't want relationships with your brand, so they shouldn't be forced.
- *Spending too much on customers who are unavailable*: these people have to move from strongly to weakly unavailable through ambivalence to being available. This road can be too long and unrealistic.
- *Spending according to value instead of commitment*: relationship managers are wrong to lavish attention just on high-value customers who are already very committed.
- *Inadequate management at point of purchase*: uncommitted users do not go out of their way to find brands, which means your communication strategy could be as simple as making the product clearly available.

- *Believing that advertising can change perceptions*: advertising actually works best at reinforcing current beliefs.
- *Too much advertising*: many brands spend far too much and annoy potential customers through saturation.
- *Too little advertising*: conversely, people can't consider your product if they aren't aware of it.
- *Unnecessary price-cutting*: this erodes the total brand equity in the market and seldom results in long-term share increases.
- *Unnecessary new product development*: ignoring commitment to existing brands overestimates the success of new ones.

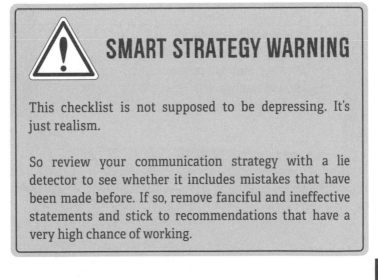

SMART STRATEGY WARNING

This checklist is not supposed to be depressing. It's just realism.

So review your communication strategy with a lie detector to see whether it includes mistakes that have been made before. If so, remove fanciful and ineffective statements and stick to recommendations that have a very high chance of working.

SMART COMMUNICATION STRATEGY SUMMARY

- Say less for more impact.
- Use polite directness.
- Give it social currency.
- Disadvantage can be advantage.
- Do things and tell people.
- Mind your language.
- Review and learn from mistakes.

SMART STRATEGY SCRAMBLER

This book has dealt with strategy in seven areas, but in truth, many of the ideas are transferable. So, if you are looking for inspiration on any topic, let your eyes wander across this spread and steal something inspiring.

- Strategy is choice.
- Think before you plan.
- Pursue principles, not money.
- Widen your options and attain distance.
- Remove silos.
- Uncommon sense vs. common nonsense.
- Find your NEMO.
- Is there a market in the gap?
- Investigate the uninteresting.
- Change the problem.
- Doubt everything.
- Messiness = unexpected links.
- Most things aren't worth doing.
- Copy something.
- Your research could be misleading you.
- Is there a thinking/doing gap?
- Are your customers really loyal?
- Are they really satisfied?

- Don't panic: service recovery can be beneficial.
- Customers make strange decisions.
- Small changes can have a disproportionately big effect.
- Selling isn't just for salespeople.
- Successful selling means challenging.
- Try rational drowning.
- Beware the hammock.
- New business could come from existing business.
- Weird is the new normal.
- Close the strategy/execution gap.
- Manage the people, not the numbers.
- Think clearly, then act courageously.
- Ensure organizational health.
- Get people in flow.
- Foster trust and teamwork.
- Everyone can master something.
- Harness the power of clevers.
- Work at the crossroads between creativity and commerce.
- SIT and audit.
- See your business as a service.
- Make your luck.
- Compete on all fronts at once.
- Overcome the fraught first mile.
- Keep it frugal.
- Say less for more impact.
- Use polite directness.
- Give it social currency.
- Disadvantage can be advantage.
- Do things and tell people.
- Mind your language.
- Review and learn from mistakes.

DRAWING IT ALL TOGETHER: A MANIFESTO FOR SMART STRATEGY

PART ONE: COMMERCIAL STRATEGY

Business Genius, James Bannerman (Pearson, 2014)
Business Is Beautiful, Jean-Baptiste Danet et al. (LID, 2013)
Decisive, Chip & Dan Heath (Random House, 2013)
Essentialism, Greg McKeown (Virgin, 2014)
Playing to Win, Alan G. Lafley & Roger Martin (Harvard Business Review Press, 2013)
The Silo Effect, Gillian Tett (Little Brown, 2015)
The Strategy Book, Max McKeown (Pearson, 2012)
Uncommon Sense, Common Nonsense, Jules Goddard & Tony Eccles (Profile, 2012)

PART TWO: BRAND STRATEGY

Copy, Copy, Copy, Mark Earls (Wiley, 2015)
Essentialism, Greg McKeown (Virgin Books, 2014)
Messy, Tim Harford (Little, Brown, 2016)
One Plus One Equals Three, Dave Trott (Macmillan, 2015)
Predatory Thinking, Dave Trott (Macmillan, 2013)
Thinking, Fast and Slow, Daniel Kahneman (Allen Lane, 2011)
Thinking in New Boxes, Luc de Brabandere & Alan Iny (Random House, 2013)
Where Good Ideas Come From, Steven Johnson (Penguin, 2010)

PART THREE: CUSTOMER STRATEGY
Commitment-Led Marketing, Jan Hendrik Hofmeyr & Butch Rice (Wiley, 2001)
Consumer.ology, Philip Graves (Nicholas Brealey, 2013)
Decoded, Phil Barden (Wiley, 2013)
The Effortless Experience, Matthew Dixon, Nick Toman & Rick DeLisi (Portfolio Penguin, 2013)
Nudge, Richard H. Thaler & Cass R. Sunstein (Caravan, 2008)
The Reputation Book, Guy Arnold & Russell Wood (LID, 2017)
The Small Big, Steve Martin, Noah Goldstein & Robert Cialdini (Profile, 2014)

PART FOUR: SALES STRATEGY
The Brand Gap, Marty Neumeier (New Riders, 2006)
The Challenger Sale, Matthew Dixon & Brent Adamson (Portfolio Penguin, 2011)
Conversations that Win the Complex Sale, Erik Peterson & Tim Riesterer (McGraw Hill, 2011)
Essentialism, Greg McKeown (Virgin Books, 2014)
To Sell Is Human, Daniel Pink (Canongate, 2012)
We Are All Weird, Seth Godin (Portfolio Penguin, 2015)

PART FIVE: PEOPLE STRATEGY

The Advantage, Patrick Lencioni (Josey-Bass, 2012)
Clever, Rob Goffee & Gareth Jones (Harvard Business Press, 2009)
Drive, Daniel Pink (Canongate, 2009)
The Five Dysfunctions of a Team, Patrick Lencioni (Josey-Bass, 2002)
Flow, Mihaly Csikszentmihalyi (Rider, 2002)
Grit, Angela Duckworth (Vermillion, 2017)
The Ideal Team Player, Patrick Lencioni (Josey-Bass, 2016)
Leaders Eat Last, Simon Sinek (Portfolio Penguin, 2014)
Left Brain, Right Stuff, Phil Rosenzweig (Profile, 2014)
Mastery, Robert Greene (Profile, 2012)

PART SIX: INNOVATION STRATEGY

Big Bang Disruption, Larry Downes & Paul Nunes
(Portfolio Penguin, 2014)
The First Mile, Scott D. Anthony (Harvard Business
Review Press, 2014)
Frugal Innovation, Navi Radjou & Jaideep Prabhu
(Economist Books, 2015)
How to Kill a Unicorn, Mark Payne (Nicholas Brealey, 2014)

Inside the Box, Jacob Goldenberg & Drew Boyd (Profile, 2013)
The Little Black Book of Innovation, Scott D. Anthony
(Harvard Business Review Press, 2011)
Open Services Innovation, Henry Chesbrough (Wiley, 2011)
The Science of Serendipity, Matt Kingdon (Wiley, 2012)
Thinking in New Boxes, Luc de Brabandere & Alan Iny
(Random House, 2013)

PART SEVEN: COMMUNICATION STRATEGY
A Beautiful Constraint, Adam Morgan & Mark Barden
(Wiley, 2015)
Brief, Joseph McCormack (Wiley, 2014)
Business Genius, James Bannerman (Pearson, 2014)
Commitment-Led Marketing, Jan Hendrik Hofmeyr & Butch Rice
(Wiley, 2001)
Contagious, Jonah Berger (Simon & Schuster, 2013)
David and Goliath, Malcolm Gladwell (Penguin Allen Lane, 2013)
The Language of Leaders, Kevin Murray (Kogan Page, 2012)
Paid Attention, Faris Yakob (Kogan Page, 2015)
When Cultures Collide, Richard Lewis (Nicholas Brealey, 2006)

ABOUT THE AUTHOR

KEVIN DUNCAN is a business adviser, marketing expert, motivational speaker and best-selling author. After 20 years in advertising and direct marketing, he has spent the last 20 years as an independent troubleshooter, advising companies how to change their businesses for the better.

Contact the author for advice, training or speaking opportunities:
kevinduncanexpertadvice@gmail.com
@kevinduncan
expertadviceonline.com
thesmartstrategybook.com

Also by the author:
Business Greatest Hits
How To Run and Grow Your Own Business
How To Tame Technology and Get Your Life Back
Marketing Greatest Hits
Marketing Greatest Hits Volume 2
Revolution
Run Your Own Business
Small Business Survival
So What?
Start
Start Your Own Business
The Bullshit-Free Book
The Business Bullshit Book
The Diagrams Book
The Excellence Book
The Ideas Book
The Intelligent Work Book
The Smart Thinking Book
Tick Achieve
What You Need To Know About Starting A Business